opposing viewpoints®
SOURCES

foreign policy

1988 annual

David L. Bender, *Publisher*
Bruno Leone, *Executive Editor*
M. Teresa O'Neill, *Senior Editor*
Bonnie Szumski, *Senior Editor*
Janelle Rohr, *Senior Editor*
Lynn Hall, *Editor*
Susan Bursell, *Editor*
Julie S. Bach, *Editor*
Thomas Modl, *Editor*
William Dudley, *Editor*
Robert C. Anderson, *Editor*

greenhaven press, inc.
San Diego, CA

ISBN 0-89908-537-7
ISSN 0748-2841

contents

"On the basis of what [Aquino] . . . has done already and the crises she has survived, I believe she is up to the job."

The Aquino Presidency Is Strong

Stephen W. Bosworth

Since I returned from my assignment in the Philippines, I have repeatedly been asked one question about Philippine President Corazon Aquino: "Can she make it?"

Initially, I responded with a nod and a brief "I believe she can." In the wake of the recent [August 28, 1987] military coup attempt, however, the question requires a more complete response. First, the question itself requires definition. If "making it" means turning the Philippines into a stable, prosperous, self-confident model of democracy in a developing country, the answer is clearly no. The problems are too difficult, the Philippine sense of nationhood too weak, and the time given to Aquino until of the end of her term in 1992 too short.

On the other hand, if the question is whether her government can survive and whether she can continue to make gradual but important progress in solving the country's problems, then my answer remains, "I believe she can."

The Real Question

I sometimes sense, however, that the real question being asked is not so much "can she make it" but "is she really up to it?" Is this sincere and courageous woman strong enough and tough enough to prevail against the forces arrayed against her—communists, aggressive colonels and political warlords?

Again, having watched her at first hand during the first year of her presidency, my answer is, "Yes, I believe she is." On the basis of what she has done already and the crises she has survived, I believe she is up to the job. She is no longer the inexperienced housewife—as she was described by Ferdinand Marcos, and by herself, during the election campaign nearly two years ago.

Aquino has surprised many people over the past several months, including some of those who originally supported her against Marcos. Throughout the election campaign and in the first months of her presidency, many of the more experienced politicians in her camp assumed that she would reign but not rule and that they would run the country.

Misreading Aquino

This proved to be a fundamental misreading of Corazon Aquino. She is intelligent and tough-minded. She was tempered by the election campaign and by her successful leadership of the Filipino people during the dramatic events that followed the election and that culminated in Marcos' flight from Manila.

However, the first months in office were difficult for her. Not only did she have no experience in public administration, but she also had the handicap of never having been a working woman, of never having had to assert herself in a day-to-day working environment. She had to learn to impose her personal leadership on a diverse collection of ambitious men and women, many of whom had political agendas not compatible with her own.

Moreover, she did not have the advantage of being the head of a political party with an even partially thought-out and coherent program of government. Rather, she was the leader of an amorphous national movement, consisting of competing political parties, single-issue groups, the church and the modern business community. In terms of political ideology these groups ranged from right-of-center to the noncommunist left. The only thing that had brought these diverse constituencies together was a shared antipathy to Marcos.

Once in power, however, the movement had no agreed-upon agenda and there had been no transition period in which to develop one. On Saturday afternoon they were organizing protest rallies against Marcos; the following Tuesday they

Stephen W. Bosworth, "Can Aquino Make It?" *Washington Post National Weekly Edition*, October 12, 1987. © The Washington Post.

were in power.

But Aquino has been the president of the Philippines [since February 1986]. She has become an experienced administrator and decision-maker. She has wrestled with the politics of choosing a Cabinet and then reshuffling that Cabinet. She has prepared a national budget, with all the difficult trade-offs among political constituencies and national priorities that are inevitable for a government painfully short of money. She has largely neutralized the diehard Marcos supporters and forced the resignation of her first minister of national defense, Juan Ponce Enrile.

Yet in the West, and even in the Philippines, Aquino is sometimes seen as a cautious leader, perhaps too cautious. She is criticized for not having taken advantage of her popular support to attack more vigorously the country's critical problems. Filipinos, of course, have a legitimate right to offer their president criticism and advice. It is their country, and free speech and a free press are, after all, guaranteed by the new constitution.

Different Cultures

However, we, the United States, should be wary of giving Aquino advice, no matter how sincere our intentions. What may seem to us to be excessive caution must be viewed within a national culture in which compromise is valued over confrontation and risk is avoided whenever possible.

We should also remember that Aquino believes deeply that she did not become president in order to continue the recent tradition of one-person rule in the Philippines. If the Philippines is to be a functioning democracy, she argues, the people should accept responsibility for their national destiny, and national policies should be made through the decisions of democratic institutions, not by presidential decree.

"We have a powerful national interest in the success of the Aquino government."

Aquino has recognized from the outset of her administration how fragile the Filipino sense of nationhood is. I believe it is this recognition, reinforced by her own instinct, that has caused her to stress national reconciliation and the healing of the wounds left by Marcos. These beliefs, not a weakness of personal leadership, dictated her response to the first several efforts to destabilize her government and until recently governed her approach toward the problems in the military.

Widespread poverty and hundreds of years of colonial rule in the Philippines also make her job particularly difficult. For many people, particularly in the rural Philippines, the central government—any central government—is perceived as an alien presence that collects taxes and imposes a legal system irrelevant and insensitive to local concerns.

This situation was exacerbated in the last years of the Marcos regime. The effective reach of the national government atrophied as a result of corruption and the concentration of national authority in Manila. The quality of public services, such as education, medical treatment, roads and security deteriorated sharply. Too many people came to see the central government and its military not as their protector, but as their antagonist. All this further weakened the already tenuous Filipino sense of nationhood. Not surprisingly, it also led to rapid growth in grass-roots support for the communist-led New People's Army.

Problems Remain

Aquino has accomplished much, but critical problems remain. The country is desperately poor. Even if the current rate of economic growth of about 5 percent to 6 percent a year is sustained for the [next] several years, per-capita incomes will not climb back to the level of the late 1970s until the early 1990s. In effect, the Philippines has lost 10 years. The problem of its $28 billion foreign debt is being managed, but it remains a heavy burden on a weak economy.

So, what can the United States do? First, we should continue doing what we have been doing: make unequivocally clear our full support for the Aquino government. No group that contemplates the overthrow of the Aquino government should have any reason to hope to receive any economic and military assistance from the United States. We have a powerful national interest in the success of the Aquino government.

But factionalism and discontent within the armed forces of the Philippines will not stop just because the United States wishes them to stop. They will stop only when professionalism is restored within the institution, when tension and suspicion between the government and the armed forces have been reduced, and when the military is confident about itself and its proper role in the Philippines. This is a task for Filipinos. Officers and civilians alike must work to build a sense of mutual confidence and trust.

America Should Help

The United States can and should help, however. Fortunately, the situation is far from hopeless. Even under Marcos, many Filipino officers remained committed to the principles of professionalism, even if they were frustrated in their attempts to operate on such principles. Also, notwithstanding the recent coup attempt, the Philippine military is already a better military, more professional and better led.

Much more remains to be done, however, and given the financial crisis that continues to grip the Aquino government, the only realistic source for the sort of money required for a major effort to rebuild the military is the United States. The military assistance we are providing, about $100 million per year, is barely enough to prevent a further deterioration in the capabilities of the Philippine armed forces. If we want to act on our concern for the future of democracy in the Philippines—and our concern over the threat from the communist insurgency—we should move immediately to provide substantially more military aid. In the final analysis, however, the future of democracy in the Philippines will depend on the Filipino people. They will have to continue to manifest their own unequivocal commitment to democratic, civilian rule. Their popular will is the most powerful antidote to any spreading of political adventurism within the military.

Stephen W. Bosworth was the US ambassador to the Philippines from 1984 to 1987.

"President Aquino has lost a good deal of the political center and has made concessions after every attempted coup."

The Aquino Presidency Is Weak

Erhard Haubold

Philippine President Corazon Aquino will serve out her full term and stay in office until 1992, says one person. No, says the next, there will be another coup, and Vice President Salvador Laurel, the islands' greatest political chameleon, has declared himself ready for her job.

U.S. ambassador Nicholas Platt is, like Secretary of State George Shultz, bullish about the future of the former American colony. But the CIA and Defense Department have little use for Corazon Aquino; for them, she is too soft in her fight against communist guerrillas, and has yet to say yes to the renewal of the treaty granting the U.S. bases there.

The Aquino Government

Can nothing prevent this Southeast Asian nation from being seen in the West as a crisis-riddled, unstable, poor land full of guns and private armies? In a week without an attempted coup, the Manila stock exchange index soars; that is how limited expectations are after two years of the Aquino government.

"If only the coup attempts would end," say the people in the slums, where, as the widow of a martyr, Aquino continues to enjoy unlimited respect. She has a good heart, she is a virtuous woman, and of course she knows nothing of the bulldozer brigades that the police continue to send to destroy their shacks. They insist she also knows nothing of the nation's widespread corruption, and nothing of its nepotism (gambling and import licenses have supposedly been given to the president's brother and sister-in-law).

It is true that Aquino is more relaxed than former ruler Ferdinand Marcos was in wielding power, but there is no major intellectual thrust to her rule, no effort to accelerate social and political change. "She

Erhard Haubold, "Who's In Charge In Manila?" *Frankfurter Allgemeine Zeitung,* reprinted in *World Press Review,* February 1988. Reprinted with permission.

remains simply an officeholder," writes one of the most respected editors in the country, Amando Doronila of the *Manila Chronicle.*

No one believes the daily announcements from the army that claim victories over the communists and Moslem separatists, nor their figures on their own losses. Occasionally one learns that, in fact, the troops got into firefights with the police, that most of those captured are petty criminals, and that the brave soldiers that Cory Aquino congratulates on her infrequent visits to the army have been disarmed in advance by the presidential security guards.

Is the military satisfied with the 60-percent raise for the troops? A colonel laughs and pulls out a wad of 100-peso notes, each the average monthly salary [$4.82] of a private. For an officer, the official salary is a minor part of his income. Forty percent of all gambling—casinos and cock-fights—is controlled by the armed forces.

Puffed Up Achievements

The campaigns against the communists in Bicol, launched with so much publicity, have been "puffed up," the government admits, because the local governor needed to win the next election. Five bridges have been blown up in the strategic province surrounding the capital, and the rebel New People's Army (NPA) announces that only two of these were their work, insinuating that the other three were blown up by the army—perhaps to scare the politicians in Manila? That would point to Chief of Staff Fidel Ramos, upon whom Aquino is even more dependent since the last coup attempt in August [1987].

During that rebellion, in which soldiers, rich "cousins" of Marcos, and their private armies participated along with many top conservative opposition figures, there was no talk of such concepts as loyalty or mutiny. Instead, the president took seriously the suggestion made by Laurel that she negotiate with the rebellion's leader, Col. Gregorio Honasan [who was later captured and dismissed from the army]. Defense Secretary Raphael Ileto said that he did not want to justify the actions of those soldiers who took part in the coup, but that they had "strengthened the morale of the anti-communist groups within the armed forces." He continued, "We would like to fight with them against our common foe."

One university professor believes that "a historical compromise based on anti-communism" is in the works, a "capitulation to the extreme right." If Aquino permits this, it will mean an end to the democratic freedom that people struggled for before and after the fight against Marcos. It would also put the "legal left," including many of her present advisers, in danger.

Movement to the Right

Things have not gone this far yet, but there is no doubt that President Aquino has lost a good deal of the political center and has made concessions after every attempted coup. "Leftish" cabinet ministers have been dismissed, and there have been no prosecutions for human rights violations that occurred during the Marcos government. In these areas, the president is responding to pressure from her opponents and possibly also from the Americans. But she has also followed her own political instincts.

She is the daughter of a rich family (co-owners of the largest sugar plantation in the islands). The left complains that she fears mass movements, has little to say to the very poor, and sees poverty overwhelmingly as a problem for charity. The left asks why she has not at least done something about land reform—her most important single campaign promise—while she still has special powers, rather than leaving it to Congress, which operates slowly and has a membership that is 80 percent wealthy.

"There are complaints about the 'educated housewife's' political naiveté."

The militant left announced to Aquino that she was not invited to the burial of Leandro Alejandro, the leftist leader murdered in September [1987], although 100,000 people attended. The left will no longer go out into the streets for her; that was clear during the latest coup attempt, when "people power" could not even mobilize 10,000 demonstrators. The major leftist labor and farmers' organizations have distanced themselves from the president, accusing their erstwhile heroine of not "standing up for the ordinary people," of not being able to overcome her class background.

Even the liberals and the middle class, the former members of the "yellow brigades" and the "congress of the streets" now criticize Aquino. She succeeded in getting a new constitution, winning a plebiscite, and forming a Congress, but has not been able to fill the empty political middle ground with a program of her own, they say. Virtue is not policy, and flowers and hymns will not bring the communists to the bargaining table.

There are complaints about the "educated housewife's" political naiveté. It is said that she was never on the right track; it was just that given the importance of removing Marcos, which was her great service, no one noticed it. She lacks the will to make spontaneous decisions, will not visit villages (the budget for this has not been used), and tends toward an "invisible" presidency. She avoids the pressing of the flesh so important in the Philippines. The most recent opinion polls point to her loss of popularity.

The breakdown of peace talks with the NPA at the beginning of 1987 is widely seen as a turning point in Aquino's presidency. Since then, there has been less talk of reforms, and more of militarization. The head of state has generally been forced to react to initiatives from underground forces, whose "sparrows" (urban terrorists) have attacked not just the police in Manila, but also U.S. soldiers and business people. Neither side was especially interested in the peace negotiations, and neither sent its top leaders there. . . .

Obstacles to Reform

The forces arrayed against Aquino include former Defense Minister Juan Ponce Enrile, now a senator. He is wealthy and respected, and has excellent connections to the rebellious officers. There are the people, inside and outside of the armed forces, who are financed by Marcos. In Ilocos Norte, the former dictator's home province, they have recruited a solid bloc of soldiers. There are the people around chief of staff Fidel Ramos, whom the well-off businessmen would like to see at the nation's helm, guaranteeing stability.

One can only speculate about American interests and their weight. They do not want to see the most important American base outside of the U.S. moved to another country.

The middle class' political honeymoon with Aquino is over, but the liberals and intellectuals do not want to give up, for they know what is at stake. It is still not too late for social reforms, but obviously they must be drastic. Aquino must finally put forth a program for social justice and national independence, a vision that can nourish her people's hopes.

Erhard Haubold is a German journalist.

"U.S. sea power in the region is of paramount importance to the economic and security interests not only of the U.S. itself, but also of the Philippines."

viewpoint **3**

The US Should Maintain Its Military Presence in the Philippines

Ferdinand Marcos

For the first time since the end of the Second World War, the United States finds itself facing a credible naval challenge in East Asia. Soviet maritime forces now have access to four naval bases in Vietnam and Kampuchea. Soviet submarines, missile-capable battle cruisers, and light aircraft carriers have used these port facilities, and twenty to thirty Soviet naval combat and support vessels regularly use Camranh Bay. These maritime forces are supported by seven major airfields in Laos and Vietnam. Soviet aircraft make reconnaissance sweeps over the South China Sea as far east as Philippine airspace. At the same time, growing Soviet contacts with Kiribati, Vanuatu, and Papua New Guinea . . . all suggest that the strategic balance in the South Pacific is under considerable pressure.

To offset this Soviet presence and maintain a deterrent balance in the region, the United States must have access to local onshore support facilities. For that purpose, the Philippine bases have always been critical. If the United States lost access to the facilities in the Philippines, it would have to move its forces to the east and north. Tinian, Palau, and Saipan have been suggested; however, not only would they be some considerable distance from the critical ship passages of the South China Sea, but facilities would still have to be constructed. Labor and supplies would have to be imported at very high cost, and construction of adequate facilities would probably take about a decade—and even then the facilities would not compare with those already available at Subic and Clark in the Philippines. In short, too little, too late.

U.S. sea power in the region is of paramount importance to the economic and security interests not only of the U.S. itself, but also of the Philippines

and all the other trade-oriented nations of East Asia. Because of the long security relationship with the United States, the armed forces of the Philippines have never been charged with sealane-defense missions. The unique contribution of the Philippines to the security of the region has been that of making facilities available to U.S. forces in a strategically important locale. The arrangement thus provided the Philippines with cost-effective security; the United States with communications, intelligence, command, logistics, ship-repair, and training facilities in a critical region of the world; and the ASEAN [Association of Southeast Asian Nations] nations with the stability that allowed the economies of Thailand, Malaysia, Singapore, and Indonesia to grow as rapidly as they have.

Pre-Aquino Philippine governments understood all of this, and allowed the renewal of base agreements without demanding compensation or concessions. With each renewal, the U.S. President pledged only to make his "best effort" to obtain economic-assistance funds and some military-aid grants. In comparison to concessions demanded by, say, Greece, Spain, or Portugal, the Philippines asked little of the United States.

The Aquino Problem

It is a security connection between allied sovereign nations, calculated to serve the best interests of both. That is, it *was*, until the ascension of Corazon Aquino in February 1986 broke the continuity of the Republic of the Philippines. The coup came at a time when the Philippine-U.S. Bases Agreement (which is scheduled to terminate in 1991) was up for renegotiation.

Few Americans seem prepared to consider the difficulties that will attend the next attempt to renew the Philippine-bases agreement. Indeed, few Americans seem prepared to seriously consider the larger implications of the new administration in

Manila, both for U.S. and for Philippine security.

Corazon Aquino has been remarkably explicit—if not wholly consistent—about her opposition to continued U.S. access to military facilities in the Philippines. Early in her campaign against my administration, she announced her opposition to the presence of "foreign troops" on Philippine soil. In December 1984, she crafted a "Unity Platform" to bring together all the political opposition to the established government of the Philippines at that time. Article 3.6 of that platform (which was subsequently published as *A Declaration of Unity*) states: "Foreign military bases on Philippine territory must be removed, and no foreign military bases shall hereafter be allowed." Among those who signed the document were Jovito Salonga, now President of the new Philippine Senate, and Representative Ramon Mitra, now Speaker of the new House of Representatives. Those whom Mrs. Aquino gathered around herself include many other signatories to the Unity Platform, such as the late Jaime V. Ongpin, who served as Secretary of Finance; Aquilino Pimentel, formerly Minister of Local Government, who now serves in the Philippine legislature; and Raul Manglapus, Minister of Foreign Affairs.

"United States withdrawal from the Philippines would significantly alter the balance of power in Southeast Asia."

When Corazon Aquino put together the team charged with the responsibility of writing a new constitution for the Republic of the Philippines, she knew perfectly well what they would produce. In Article 18, Section 25 of the "temporary provisions" of the Aquino constitution, we find the following:

> After the expiration in 1991 of the Agreement between the Republic of the Philippines and the United States of America concerning Military Bases, foreign military bases, troops, or facilities shall not be allowed in the Philippines except under a treaty duly concurred in by the Senate and, when the Congress so requires, ratified by a majority of the votes cast by the people in a national referendum held for that purpose.

By including such provisions in her constitution, Corazon Aquino has accomplished several things. On the one hand, she satisfied her anti-American supporters by making it virtually impossible to renew the Philippine-U.S. Bases Agreement. The present members of the new Philippine Senate are scheduled to hold office for six years—until after the current bases agreement has expired. According to the new constitution, a ratification of any treaty renewing the bases would require confirmation by two-thirds of the 24 senators. A recent survey of Philippine senators showed less than half the required number supporting a new treaty.

The last surveys of public opinion collected during my administration indicated that a plurality of voters—about 40 per cent of those responding to the query—favored the continuation of U.S. access to Philippine facilities. About 30 per cent of respondents were opposed to the continued presence of the U.S. forces; that left 30 per cent undecided. Which means that only if the government made a strong case in support of a new treaty could it hope to win a national referendum on the issue.

Given the prevailing disposition of the leadership in Manila, this will not happen. And yet Corazon Aquino will be free to tell her American critics that final termination of the Philippine-U.S. Bases Agreement reflects, not her choice, but the will of the Philippine people. She has established the grounds for what Americans nowadays like to call "plausible denial."

Altering the Balance of Power

United States withdrawal from the Philippines would significantly alter the balance of power in Southeast Asia, to the detriment of the future security of South Korea, Japan, Taiwan—even the People's Republic of China. The response time of U.S. armed forces to any crisis in the South China Sea would be measurably increased. The greater distances involved would reduce the on-station time of U.S. aircraft and surface vessels throughout the region, and the diminished presence would affect local perceptions of America's credibility as a security partner. Ever since the announcement of Richard Nixon's "Guam Doctrine," with its withdrawal of U.S. forces from Southeast Asia and Taiwan, U.S. allies in the region have entertained doubts about the United States' determination and ability to defend their general interests, which the loss of access to Philippine bases could only exacerbate. Certainly the loss of forward bases in the area would make defense of the sealanes manifestly more difficult and increasingly expensive.

The Future of the Philippines

Of course, Mrs. Aquino and her entourage may not be able to remain in control of the situation in the Philippines until 1991. For one thing, the most sanguine estimates are that the Philippine economy will enjoy only modest real growth over the next four or five years. Unemployment will increase and poverty will become more pervasive, improving the recruitment opportunities of the radical Left. Guerrilla activity in the countryside will probably intensify.

The survival of the Aquino administration under such conditions will be very problematic, for unlike prior administrations it will have great difficulty in dealing with enemies on the Left. Before the 1986 coup, the Aquino opposition made extensive use of radical students, disaffected neo-Marxist intellectuals, "progressive" clerics, and left-wing "nationalists." All these groups entertained some variant of Marxism as central to their beliefs, and many of them provided members of the new government. Administration members Joker Arroyo, the late Jose Diokno, and Lorenzo Tanada, among many others, represent the tendentious anti-Americanism and overtly leftist orientation of the Aquino administration.

Because of these political debts to the Left, Corazon Aquino, once she was in power, offered an unconditional amnesty to all political offenders. The arrangement granted amnesty to Marxist-Leninist-Maoist criminals who were guilty of murdering members of the national-security forces, civilian functionaries, and ordinary citizens. It extended immunity to leftist terrorists, as well as to felons who had extorted "revolutionary taxes" from all and sundry.

While murderers and felons were being granted unconditional amnesty, the Aquino administration gave Jose Diokno the job of prosecuting members of the military who were charged with human-rights violations. In other words, those who had taken up arms against the state were granted unconditional amnesty, but members of the armed forces of the Philippines were made subject to prosecution.

Rise of Communists

In consequence, Communist guerrilla leaders were able to become celebrities in Manila. They appeared on national television advocating an early abrogation of the security arrangement between the Philippines and the United States. By the middle of 1986, while the Philippine military protested in vain, Communist leaders had achieved star status, recruited more guerrilla fighters, and improved their communications and logistics infrastructure.

"Moscow, in fact, has already made overtures to Manila, offering substantial economic assistance."

At the same time, the Aquino administration did little to improve the fighting capacity of the armed forces. Threatened with prosecution for human-rights infractions on the one hand, and denied the material support necessary to the effective suppression of armed rebellion on the other, the Philippine military felt compelled to make its case dramatically. The result has been a series of tragic coup attempts—the surface manifestation of deep and fundamental frustrations.

As the credibility of the Aquino administration erodes, the organized "legal" Left and the armed revolutionaries in the countryside will operate increasingly from a position of strength. The prospects are that a fatally weakened Aquino government would be drawn into a coalition with the Communist Left. That would be the penultimate stage in the progression toward a revolutionary Marxist-Leninist state. Among the first acts of such an interim "national democratic" government would be the expulsion of all "foreign" military forces from the Philippine archipelago.

The Soviet Threat

Should the United States react by withdrawing economic assistance, the immediate counter-reaction would be a Philippine appeal for assistance from the Soviet bloc. Moscow, in fact, has already made overtures to Manila, offering substantial economic assistance. In this scenario, negotiations between Moscow and Manila would probably give the Soviets access to support facilities in the Philippines in exchange for general economic aid and some general security guarantees. (Many of those groups associated with the Aquino opposition before February 1986 advocated just such a policy.) In short, in exchange for a level of aid that would allow an impoverished, Cuban-style economy to survive, the Philippines would have to provide the Soviet Union the same kind of benefits extended by Hanoi and Havana.

Such developments could well presage the collapse of the U.S. defense perimeter in the Western Pacific. In the face of the consequent major Soviet expansion in Southeast Asia, Japan might well feel constrained to reassess the virtues of remaining a Western ally. The Soviet Union has already undertaken a number of initiatives designed to improve its relations with Japan. Opening its Far Eastern provinces to Japanese investment and joint ventures could be part of a long-range program for reorienting Tokyo's foreign policy in general and its security policy in particular.

At best, U.S. withdrawal from the Philippines would place the continued prosperity of the pluralistic and market-governed polities of East and Southeast Asia at risk. At worst, it could mean the expansion of the oppressive system that swallowed Kampuchea, Laos, and Vietnam. One-third of the population of Kampuchea perished at the hands of Marxist-Leninist-Maoist revolutionaries. Hundreds of thousands were compelled to flee Laos and Vietnam, scattering their dead across the vast sea spaces of Asia and the Pacific. For Americans the "Philippine crisis" is an issue of access to strategically important military facilities. For Filipinos, it may prove a matter of life and death.

Ferdinand Marcos was president of the Philippines from 1965 to 1986. He ruled under martial law from 1972 to 1981, and was defeated in a 1986 election by current president Corazon Aquino.

"I think we should gradually but definitely move out of the Philippines."

The US Should Reduce Its Military Presence in the Philippines

James Fallows

Filipinos will spend a lot of time in the next three years deciding whether American military bases should remain in their country. Since the day Corazon Aquino took office, everyone has recognized that this is the biggest foreign-policy choice her Administration will make. Assuming she serves her full term, Aquino will be in office until 1992. The Military Bases Agreement, under which the United States has stationed soldiers and sailors in the Philippines since just after the Second World War, is scheduled to expire in 1991.

Americans might well start asking themselves the same thing: whether it makes sense to leave the bases where they are. The answer might seem to be obvious. Of course we should keep bases that are so conveniently located and would be so costly and bothersome to replace. Most Filipinos—in fact, every one I've discussed the matter with—seem to take it for granted that the United States *must* have the bases. They assume that America will scratch, claw, browbeat, and bribe to protect the bases, as it has done when necessary in the past. . . .

A Dilemma

It seems to me that America's interest in the bases deserves harder thought than most Filipinos believe we'll give it. Rather than as an open-and-shut case, I think, it should be seen as another in the series of depressing dilemmas the United States faces, now that its military commitments stretch so much further than does the money to back them up. I use *dilemma* not as a mushy foreign-relations term but in its strict sense, to describe a situation in which we have two bad choices. . . .

One is to move the bases someplace else. This would be technically feasible, militarily inconvenient, financially onerous, and strategically

James Fallows, "The Bases Dilemma," *The Atlantic Monthly,* February 1988. Reprinted with the author's permission.

ominous since it would reduce the military control that is now our main source of influence in the western Pacific. The other is to hold on to the bases. This would be increasingly expensive, would link our welfare to that of the Sick Man of Asia, and would, for perverse reasons that stretch back into the Philippines' history as an American colony, postpone the moment when the Philippines gets well. . . .

The bases are convenient, cheap, already in place. It would be an expensive nuisance to move them anywhere else. But the Filipinos who dislike the bases *really* dislike them, and—if I may be permitted yet another subjective judgment—they seem to have thought more deeply about why their country is failing than those who want to keep the bases for the money they bring in. The opposition seems certain to grow. A military government might bottle it up for a while, but the only thing that could really stop it is wildly improbable. That would be a complete change in the still-colonial love-hate relationship, so that the bases were no longer part of the pathology that keeps the Philippines spiraling down. Without that change—or some other miracle—the economy will sputter and social order will deteriorate. . . .

Holding On

One choice for America is to grit our teeth and hold on. The Filipinos are unhappy? So what? Fidel Castro has been unhappy for three decades, but American Marines are at Guantanamo today. The parallel is not exact. The Philippine bases are 6,500 miles away, not a hundred, from the continental United States, and the United States enjoys long-term extra-territorial rights over Guantanamo which it lacks in the Philippines. (Many Filipinos seem unaware of these differences and suspect that if, "like Cuba," they ordered us out, we'd refuse to go.) The most likely disaster scenario for the Philippines does not involve a complete Vietnam-style Communist takeover, which would force a withdrawal from the bases. The country, with its thousands of islands, is hard for any force to sweep through, and so far neither the army nor the guerrillas seem capable of conclusively beating the other side. Instead, military observers say, disaster would probably mean fragmentation: the country could fall apart into seven or eight fiefdoms, some controlled by the Communists, others by local warlords. This would be bad for the Filipinos but not necessarily crippling to the United States. The big bases are both near Manila, the area the central government has traditionally been most able to control.

"The opposition [to the bases] seems certain to grow."

If the United States had to hold on to the bases, then, it could. It obviously has the muscle to win a test of force, and it has the money, even now, to buy the Filipinos off for a while. But does it have to hold on? What about trying to spare itself future trouble—fighting a Communist revolution, dealing with terrorists, taking moral and political responsibility for another pro-base dictator—by voluntarily moving out?

Although officials at the U.S. Embassy and at the bases patiently deflect questions about alternate sites, of course the government has been studying them. Reports from the war colleges, various universities and think tanks, and congressional offices differ in detail but agree on two main points. First, it would be harder and more expensive to do the same jobs from any other site. Second, the jobs could be done.

Other Options

That is could be done is an important starting point. If it were not so—if leaving Subic and Clark meant leaving Asia altogether—we'd have to hang on as tenaciously as the Russians do in Cuba, at least until we figured out how much of an Asian presence we, for our own reasons, wanted to maintain. There are other places to put the facilities that are now at Subic and Clark. The three options discussed in most military analyses are shifting to existing American bases (in Japan, Guam, and Hawaii); building new bases on the Micronesian islands east of the Philippines, where the United States has obtained basing rights; and making new arrangements elsewhere in Southeast Asia.

None of the options would be quite so good as Subic and Clark. Unlike any alternative, the Philippine bases are already there, and don't have to

be built from the ground up. According to a report from the Congressional Research Service, the capital value of buildings, machinery, and equipment at the two bases is slightly over $2 billion. Rebuilding the bases from the ground up would cost several times that much. Five years ago Admiral Robert Long, then the commander-in-chief of U.S. Pacific forces, estimated that it would cost $3 billion to $4 billion to shift to Guam and Micronesia. . . .

The Bases and Strategy

But once we've thought about cost, we've faced the worst news about relocating the bases. This isn't like moving out of West Berlin. The purely strategic obstacles are, in most cases, easy to overcome. Why, after all, did the United States hold on to the bases after the Second World War? Forward deployment in Asia was originally meant to contain the godless Chinese. That rationale is entirely gone. Some U.S. military studies warn that losing the bases would mean retracting America's own defense perimeter, but this is ludicrous. The only threats to America's physical security come from Soviet missiles and terrorist bombs, and the Philippine bases can't help protect us against either. In the sky's-the-limit early Reagan years, Secretary of the Navy John Lehman often talked about a Navy bold enough to take the fight directly to the Soviets, hunting them down in their home ports. None of the American Embassy or military officials I interviewed in the Philippines offered this as a justification for Subic. So why are the bases there? They have three stated functions: helping out in Northeast Asia, or Korea and Japan and the sea lanes leading there; serving as a way point for routine show-the-flag missions in the Indian Ocean and the Middle East and also supporting unusual operations like the current Persian Gulf patrol; and policing Southeast Asia as a whole, which includes defending the Philippines.

The first mission involves the most important countries but depends least on bases in the Philippines. Subic and Clark are a long way south of Japan and Korea, and the United States has large forces on the scene in both those countries. (Manila is at the same latitude as Honduras, Seoul and Tokyo at about the same as Washington.) American strategy in Korea calls for a "come as you are" defense against North Korean invasion, rather than counting on rapid reinforcement from the Philippines. A conventional invasion of Japan must be the world's least appetizing military prospect. It was dread of just such an undertaking, when Japan was already beaten to a pulp in the Second World War, that persuaded President Harry Truman to drop the atomic bombs. Japan needs some protection, and the straits that surround it need to be patrolled, but those jobs can be done by forces in Japan.

The second mission, supporting Indian Ocean and Persian Gulf operations, does depend heavily on the

Philippine bases. Subic is the hub for the Seventh Fleet, and Clark is the major trans-shipment point for men and goods going to the Gulf. Supporting the same missions without the Philippines would be more costly, but there's no strictly geographical reason why it couldn't be done. For instance, a 1986 Congressional Research Service study concluded that Micronesian bases, such as Tinian and Saipan, "would provide a relatively secure sea route . . . to the Indian Ocean through the Indonesia Straits." The Navy has sunk about $75 billion into its shipbuilding program in the past seven years—largely to make its fleet more mobile and less dependent on specific bases. What was the point, if the Navy's still hostage at Subic? The Air Force might have a bigger problem. The haul from Clark to the island of Diego Garcia, in the Indian Ocean, is 3,366 nautical miles—about as far as a transport plane can go with enough cargo to make the trip worthwhile. The Micronesian islands are about a thousand miles farther from Diego Garcia. But the trip to Diego Garcia is a thousand miles *shorter* from Singapore than from Clark, so Air Force planes starting in Micronesia could stop there or in Darwin, Australia, and reach the Indian Ocean with full payloads. The U.S. Navy already uses commercial docks in Singapore for ship repair and operates anti-submarine aircraft and tanker planes from Singapore air fields.

Defending Southeast Asia

That leaves the question of Southeast Asia, where the location of the bases does make a difference. First, they place the U.S. military on the lip of the South China Sea. When a P-3C Orion takes off from Cubi Point, it is "on-station," patrolling for Soviet submarines, virtually the instant its wheels leave the runway. A plane coming from Guam would have to spend four hours reaching its "on-station" point and four hours getting back, which wastes eight of the twelve hours it can spend in the air. Second, Subic and Clark are widely seen as counterweights to the (American-built) Soviet bases in Vietnam, at Cam Ranh Bay and Da Nang. The Soviet installations are much smaller and less valuable.

"There are other places to put the facilities that are now at Subic and Clark."

One evening in Singapore, I asked a Soviet diplomat how his government would view a bases swap—we leave the Philippines, they leave Vietnam. "Oh!" he said, nearly swallowing an ice cube in eagerness. "We would be *ready!*" Still, the Soviet bases are seen by neighboring governments as an annoyance and a potential threat. And—perhaps the most important pro-bases factor—those same governments are obviously counting on the United States to stay in the Philippines.

This attitude is vexing in several ways. Most governments refuse to be honest about it. Indonesia and Malaysia are fire-breathing "non-aligned" nations, proudly opposed to all overseas bases. Communist China can't publicly say that American bombers and warships are a constructive force. But Indonesia, Malaysia, China, and all the other countries bordering the South China Sea, except Cambodia and Vietnam, have sent unmistakable signals that they want the bases to stay. The reason is simple: removing them would upset a stable status quo that has spared most of the region the ravages of war (the noble view) and allowed it to concentrate on getting rich (the practical view). At a symposium last November [1987] in Singapore, Prime Minister Lee Kuan Yew gave a rosy (from the local perspective) forecast of Asian development into the next century and said that only three things could disturb it. One was Japanese rearmament, the second was fierce protectionism in the United States, and the third was an American departure from the Philippines.

"The underlying basis for growth since World War Two, especially in Asia, has been the stability and security provided by the United States," he said. "For several decades to come, there is no other power that can maintain the balance against the increasing presence of the Soviet navy and air force in the Far East." This he said, without drama, in his prepared speech. Then he ad libbed, with real passion, about the effect an American military withdrawal from Asia could have on the Japanese. "The most terrifying thought for me is a fundamental shift in the belief of the Japanese that the world that they have known since 1945"—that is, the world of Pax Americana in Asia—"is at an end and that they have to either depend on themselves or align themselves or come to some understanding with China or the Soviet Union. Then there is a joker in the pack."

Military Pull

The Asian attitude is irritating also because it forces Americans to confront an extremely unpleasant modern truth. It needs to be emphasized, because it's hard to accept: military power is now our principal source of influence in Asia. Now that we are borrowing money from others rather than lending it, now that our appetite for exports must shrink, the main reason that Japan, Korea, China, and others pay attention to us is that we have aircraft carriers and B-52s. Unlike the Soviet Union, the United States has other strengths, of course. The American market is still the largest, our technology is in many areas still ahead of or competitive with

Japan's, our universities are. . . clearly the most attractive in the world. But Japan now has the money that commands respect and, in Asia at least, the reputation of being tomorrow's country. The United States is listened to in large part because of the Seventh Fleet.

But if we consider the bases from America's standpoint, not Lee Kuan Yew's, even in Southeast Asia they are not indispensable. Subic and Clark may maintain America's "presence" in Southeast Asia, but in actual combat they've proved very difficult to use. The Philippine government is supposed to be consulted before the bases are used for any operation except home-island defense. This has turned into de facto veto power. During the Vietnam War, Clark would have been the logical starting point for bombing raids on Vietnam, but out of consideration for Philippine feelings the bombers left from Guam and Okinawa instead. The United States also built an expensive new B-52 base in Thailand, now abandoned, because of the difficulty of using Clark. It's hard to imagine that Southeast Asian combat will ever seem more vital to the United States than the government thought it was in the 1960s. The military made do with more-remote bases then; why not now? Moreover, Southeast Asia grows richer and more stable by the day. It may please Lee Kuan Yew and his neighbors to have us keep the peace for them indefinitely, but maybe we can't afford it anymore without help from someone else.

Pulling Out Slowly

I don't pretend to have found a way out of the dilemma. I know only, to repeat what I said at the outset, that we have two choices, both bad.

But I have a proposal for balancing vague-sounding concerns—neo-colonialism, cultural damage—against the hard strategic interests of the United States. I think we should gradually but definitely move out of the Philippines. It should be gradual so that it doesn't pull the rug out from under the Aquino government, so that it doesn't look like a panicked retreat, so that we have a chance to think calmly and carefully about what to do next. Perhaps we could bring the Russians out of Vietnam at the same time, not as an even swap but as a bonus. Perhaps we should start with the airmen and planes based at Clark, which is by all estimates easier and less costly to duplicate than Subic. Perhaps we could arrange other, less emotionally trying basing deals with other nearby countries. Raul Manglapus, the Philippine Foreign Minister, has been urging the Southeast Asian countries that benefit from the bases to share political responsibility for them. So far he's mainly flustered his neighbors, but over the years some may come around. Late last year [1987] even Malaysia's generally anti-Western Prime Minister, Mahathir bin Mohamad, said that the Philippine

bases were "necessary" as long as Russia stayed in Vietnam. Perhaps we could work on both our Asian defense dilemmas at once, convincing the Japanese that they should pay rent for bases that protect the shipments that keep them alive. Perhaps we could consider how much of an Asian presence we need to keep the peace and preserve our influence.

"The only threats to America's physical security come from Soviet missiles and terrorist bombs, and the Philippine bases can't help protect us against either."

But, even if we do it gradually, we should go. Nothing is inevitable, but more and more trouble in the Philippines is highly likely. If we stay, we'll be caught in it; if we stay, we'll help bring it on. We'll do better, with our bad choices, to make the decision ourselves rather than eventually being pushed. That can help us buy time to work out America's grand strategy for the late twentieth century: the least damaging way to withdraw from commitments we can no longer afford.

James Fallows is the Washington editor of The Atlantic Monthly.

"When the Sandinistas say they intend to take all of Central America, they mean it and are literally preparing to do so. With the help of Moscow."

Nicaragua Is a Threat to the US

William S. Armistead

On October 25, 1987, the military chief of the Communist regime in Nicaragua, Humberto Ortega, lost his personal assistant, Major Roger Miranda Bengoechea, when the major sought and received political asylum at the U.S. Embassy in Mexico City. Major Miranda's ensuing testimony about how the Soviets and Cubans planned to build an overwhelming military stronghold in Nicaragua confirmed the Leninist intentions of the ruling Ortega brothers as Miranda stripped the mask of "benign agrarian reform" from the public face of the Sandinista regime.

Miranda informed U.S. intelligence agents that three months *after* Daniel Ortega had signed Esquipulas II—the Arias peace plan—the Ortega brothers and representatives from Cuba and the Soviet Union met in Managua to design and implement a political-military strategy for Communist domination of the whole of Central America. Miranda's testimony was corroborated by Nicaraguan Defense Minister Humberto Ortega two days later, when he brazenly confirmed that the primary objectives of the Sandinista junta were the military defeat of the Democratic Resistance by 1990; comradeship in arms with the FMLN Communists against the freely elected Government of neighboring El Salvador; and, the construction of a 600,000-man Nicaraguan military. . . .

A committed Sandinista in the beginning, Miranda became disenchanted by the corruption of the Marxist-Leninists who seized power from the democratic elements in the early years of the Nicaraguan revolution. He says Humberto Ortega has a personal Swiss bank account which contained over $1,479,000 at the time of Miranda's defection. He reports that Daniel Ortega also has such an account, and that the government salaries of top Sandinista bosses are padded from under the table by "Minister of Tourism" Tomas Borge, who is in fact chief of the secret police. Meanwhile, these committed Communists are content to run a centrally planned economy with tell-tale socialist inefficiency: over 1,000 percent annual inflation, a total collapse of the export market, and thousands of desperately hungry people in the countryside. . . .

The Sandinista Tactic

Major Miranda told U.S. intelligence agents that the central thesis of President Reagan's policy in Central America has been correct all along. Miranda confirmed that the Sandinista Comandantes believe "the only way of guaranteeing the development of their Marxist programs in Nicaragua is to construct a powerful army. One can sign agreements, one can appear to be more flexible in the political system, but what will never be negotiable is the development of the Sandinista army. They know that their power rests, in the long run, in the size of that army."

According to Roger Miranda the Sandinista tactic is the same as that employed by all new Communist regimes—to stall, to negotiate coyly, and thereby dupe the West while simultaneously building their military power. The Sandinistas "don't have any desire to negotiate the size of the army that they plan to have in Nicaragua," Miranda explains. "Yes, they are going to sit down and talk. But after months of discussions they are going to say that they didn't arrive at any agreement." And Miranda *knows*.

The Communists do not rely on guns alone. They use a combination of weapons, including propaganda, deception, false treaties, and any other means available. Their most effective weapon so far has been Esquipulas II—the peace plan that won Costa Rican President Arias the Nobel Peace Prize. Major Miranda told U.S. authorities that the

William S. Armistead, "The Nicaragua Miranda Warning Our Press Ignored," *Conservative Digest*, March 1988. Reprinted with permission.

Sandinistas have no intention of honoring it. He says they have "already made an agreement with the Soviets and the Cubans about the plans for the [Sandinista] army. . . . With what desire, then, are the Sandinistas going to discuss peace when at the same time in the back of their minds they are thinking about creating one of the most powerful armies in Latin America? We are talking about self-propelled artillery, we are talking about MiG-21s, we are talking about new 400-ton ships . . . —that no other Central American country has."

When Miranda defected, he brought with him the primary document developed by the Communists at their tripartite (U.S.S.R.-Cuba-Nicaragua) conference in Havana in June 1985. Known as the "19th of July Plan," it describes in detail the intended arms buildup for the years 1986 through 1995. The plan breaks down into Land, Air, and Sea forces.

Land Forces

Keep in mind that the Sandinista army *as it stands now* is larger than all other Central American military forces *combined*. The scheduled Sandinista escalation on land between 1988 and 1990 will emphasize a buildup of troops, culminating by 1995 in a 600,000-man Sandinista army—a full 24 percent of the population under arms. That number is ten times the size of the Mexican army, and an equivalent mobilization in the United States (which now keeps less than one percent of its population under arms) would be *57 million*.

"The Sandinistas are chipping away at the North American will to prevent delivery of the high-performance fighters."

This buildup, which will occur within the first two years of the plan, will be organized into: 1 border infantry brigade, 12 unconventional warfare battalions, 49 permanent regional companies, and 1 reconnaissance battalion. For the purposes of fortifying Pacific townships, the Sandinistas plan to build 6 new light-infantry brigades: one each in Leon, Chinandega, Granada, and Masaya, and two in Managua. Also planned for the Pacific region, which contains most of the Nicaraguan population, is the deployment of 21 "Type A light infantry brigades" consisting of land-based anti-tank and anti-aircraft units. The Sandinistas plan to maintain their present force of 11 light-infantry brigades, designating them "Type B light infantry brigades."

Also to be deployed in the Pacific regions are 100 new battalions of 800 men each, to be armed with assault rifles.

Despite the relative weakness of neighboring Honduras, and Costa Rica with no army at all, the Sandinistas are promised two additional T-55 main battle-tank battalions with 31 tanks each, 122-millimeter self-propelled howitzers (by 1991), and a range of armored personnel carriers.

When the Sandinistas say they intend to take all of Central America, they mean it and are literally preparing to do so. With the help of Moscow.

Air Forces

The Sandinista buildup in air power as foreseen in the 19th of July Plan is divided into the air force, land-based communications stations, and air-defense stations. The present Sandinista air force maintains 3,500 men, six AN-26 large transport planes, at least 50 Mi-8/17 HIP armed-transport helicopters, at least 12 Soviet Mi-24/25 HIND D "flying tank" helicopters, and a 10,000-foot airstrip in Punta Huete capable of accommodating any aircraft in the Soviet-bloc inventory.

The 19th of July Plan bolsters this force substantially. It includes a squadron of MiG-21B Fishbed fighter/interceptors, which would give the Sandinistas total air superiority in the region and the ability to strike deeply inside their neighbors' territories at will. When it became known that Ortega and company were attempting to import MiGs in 1985, President Reagan wisely threatened to "take them out." Undaunted, however, the Sandinistas are chipping away at the North American will to prevent delivery of the high-performance fighters.

The plan calls for the more conventional air force to be stationed in three military regions. The first is located in Panchito, where 2 squadrons of Soviet-built Mi-17 armed-transport helicopters and 1 mixed squadron of Mi-25 HIND and Mi-8 HIP helicopters are to be deployed along with AN-2 light aircraft. The second, located in Juigalpa, is to house 1 squadron of Mi-17 helicopters, and 1 mixed squadron of Mi-25 and Mi-17 helicopters, as well as AN-2 aircraft. The third air detachment, located in Waswali, will receive the same buildup as the Juigalpa air detachment.

Included in the Soviet and Cuban plan for Nicaragua is maintenance of the heavy-transport and executive-transport systems now in place, and programs for the replacement of aircraft downed in action. In other words, numbers we have been quoting refer not to a stockpile to be withered down by attrition in battle, but numbers that are to be maintained by a constant transport of Communist Bloc arms as they are needed to maintain the Sandinista fighting force.

The second part of the proposed Sandinista air triad calls for establishment of a sophisticated infrastructure of 7 ground-based communications centers, one of which will be mobile.

The final arm of the Sandinista air strategy is the

air-defense system. One C-125 anti-aircraft rocket regiment will be added to the existing anti-aircraft artillery: 1 medium- and small-caliber artillery regiment will be added to 2 smaller-caliber anti-aircraft regiments in Managua.

We are talking here about the Soviets and Cubans creating a world-class air power in tiny Nicaragua with the capability both of striking the United States and providing and protecting Soviet bases on the American mainland. Think about it.

"The argument that the Sandinista army is defensive in nature is ridiculous when you compare it to the other forces in Central America."

The Sandinista naval buildup is to take place primarily between 1991 and 1995, and will include ships with 400-ton displacements, 1,500-mile ranges, and 57-millimeter artillery. Also included are squadrons of: 40- to 50-ton patrol boats; minesweepers (2 or 3 per squadron); and, light hydrofoils (2 or 3 per squadron). This naval buildup will include radio communications and repair bases.

A Threat to Neighbors

The cumulative effect of such a Sandinista buildup is staggering. A military analyst detailed to the State Department told *Conservative Digest* that a 600,000-man Sandinista army supported by HIND attack helicopters and MiG fighters would be able to "crush its Central American neighbors. And it would also give the Sandinistas a free hand to train and supply the Communist FMLN guerrillas fighting the democratic Government in El Salvador and to activate the dormant Communist groups in Costa Rica." When asked what the Sandinista buildup would mean should the United States have to intervene once it is in place, the analyst replied: "It would take the might of the entire U.S. military to defeat a force of 600,000. That's over twice the enemy force we faced in Vietnam. The large-caliber artillery and tanks the Sandinistas are acquiring cannot be taken into the jungle and are of little use against guerrillas. They are, however, quite useful in intimidating neighbors. The American people ought to know that the Sandinista buildup as planned in DIRIANGEN 1 and 2 [the 19th of July Plan] is not defensive, as the Sandinistas are saying, but offensive in nature—which clearly indicates that the Sandinistas have greater plans than border or internal defense."

Pedro Joaquin Chamorro, who serves on the directorate of the Nicaraguan Democratic Resistance, told *Conservative Digest* that Salvadoran President José Napoleón Duarte assured him personally that the Sandinistas have continued to supply the FMLN against his democratically elected Government even while they were promising direct negotiations and making token concessions to bemuse U.S. Congressmen. "The Sandinistas are determined to penetrate—however subtly—the Central American democracies," Chamorro advised. "As it stands now, they are isolated by the democracies and they have no allies. Their only asset is their ability to make war and to militarize the civil enemies of their neighbors. If the U.S. Congress were to abandon the Resistance, the Sandinistas would be free to consolidate their power, support the FMLN in El Salvador, and activate the dormant Communists in Costa Rica—the activists in the [labor] unions and others they have trained militarily." Still, Chamorro believes that "the majority of U.S. Congressmen want democracy for Nicaragua, and all of Central America, they just don't understand how of get it."

Be Warned

The willingness of liberals in Congress to discount the Sandinista military buildup as just a defense against fear of "Yankee imperialist forces in the field" is not only a dangerous evasion, but it ignores the whole history of Communist revolution. Congressman Connie Mack (R.-Florida), a staunch supporter of the Democratic Resistance, told *Conservative Digest*: "Daniel Ortega has assured the world that even if the Sandinistas are defeated in an election, they will never give up power—and 'power' to Communists is military power." Congressman Mack sees and says the truth:

"The argument that the Sandinista army is defensive in nature is ridiculous when you compare it to the other forces in Central America. Not only is the Sandinista military force larger than all other Central American forces combined, but it appears to indicate they are ready to move toward aggression. Ortega has no intention of working toward democracy: His desire to build a 600,000-man army from a population of 2.5 million people, and his refusal to recognize any electoral process that might result in his defeat by the Nicaraguan people, [are] clear indications he is insincere about peace and democracy."

Major Roger Miranda is reported to have chuckled when he heard Mikhail Gorbachev "talking about peace and disarmament" during the [1987] U.S./U.S.S.R. Summit in Washington. He knew that, as the smiling Gorbachev spoke, the Soviet Union was delivering to the Sandinistas the last of what amounted to $450 million in war matériel in 1987 alone. Since 1979, the value of the arms shipped to Nicaragua from the Communist Bloc has exceeded $2 billion.

Major Miranda has warned us that Daniel Ortega will build his army, that he will feign negotiations until the Resistance is disarmed, and that he will support Communist guerrillas to destabilize the Central American democracies. We have been amply warned. The question now is whether we have even a fraction of the moral and political courage that Major Miranda and the Nicaraguan Resistance have shown in trying to bring democracy to Nicaragua. If we lack vision and courage, the resulting betrayal and unjust peace will in time allow a Communist military buildup that will require our involvement in a major war on the American mainland.

William S. Armistead is a contributing editor to Conservative Digest.

"The Sandinistas, given the history of their country, are convinced that ultimately they will have to confront American military forces directly."

The US Is a Threat to Nicaragua

Alexander Cockburn and William M. LeoGrande

Editor's note: Part I of the following viewpoint is by Alexander Cockburn. Part II is by William M. LeoGrande.

I

On December 15, [1987] leaders of the House of Representatives, who only days earlier had said that there was no way the *contras* would get any more of the taxpayers' money, confided that some measure of aid to the *contras* was inevitable. They did not, naturally, admit at the same time that such aid is entirely incompatible with the Guatemala, or "Arias," accords signed by the Central American nations on August 7, [1987] and supposedly supported by the Reagan Administration.

Their change of stance must plainly be ascribed to the Administration's propaganda coup concerning the Nicaraguan defector Roger Miranda Bengoechea, formerly an assistant to Nicaraguan Defense Minister Humberto Ortega. Those big headlines of December 13 and 14 about "secret" Nicaraguan plans for a "massive" buildup have had their effect on the gossamer resolve of Congress.

What Miranda Revealed

So what do Miranda's statements chiefly amount to? He declares that:

• Nicaragua has made a long-term agreement with the Soviet Union for the provision of weapons and military aid, envisioning an eventual reduction of the standing army and an expanded popular militia;

• the Sandinistas have a secret plan to use the Guatemala accords as a "weapon" to consolidate the revolution and eliminate the *contras*;

• Nicaragua had contingency plans to expand the war to neighboring countries in the event of a U.S. invasion;

Alexander Cockburn, "Beat the Devil," *The Nation*, December 26, 1987/January 2, 1988. Reprinted with the author's permission.
William M. LeoGrande, "How to Prevent Endless War in Central America," *The New York Times*, December 18, 1987. Copyright © 1987 by The New York Times Company. Reprinted with permission.

• the war has been a drain on the Nicaraguan economy;

• the *contras* are essentially a peasant force and have made no headway in the urban centers;

• the Nicaraguan Defense Ministry keeps a secret Swiss bank account for Humberto Ortega's personal use;

• there are no more than twelve Soviet military advisers and fewer than 500 Cuban military advisers in Nicaragua;

• the Nicaraguans were training a fifteen-man group of Salvadoran guerrillas in the use of antiaircraft weapons.

The first thing to be said about Miranda's statements is that if they had been made under similar circumstances in the Soviet Union, the United States would have undoubtedly described them as part of a "propaganda offensive by the Soviet government, using the state-controlled press." Miranda was made available to a select group of reporters under carefully controlled conditions in which the chosen outlets—*The New York Times, The Washington Post, Time* and the Associated Press— agreed to a schedule of disclosure, finally pre-empted by one day by *The Post*.

This news management is reminiscent of a similar exercise engineered by Oliver North and the Office of Public Diplomacy on the night of the U.S. elections on November 6, 1984. On that occasion the nation's TV screens glowed with disclosures, which subsequently turned out to be false, that a freighter carrying "advanced Soviet MIG fighters" was nearing a Nicaraguan port and that the Reagan Administration would regard the importation of such MIGs as an unacceptable escalation by Nicaragua.

Was there anything new in what Miranda said?

Since 1980 Humberto Ortega has been calling for a firm Soviet commitment to provide substantial weaponry, including MIG fighters, but the Russians have been deaf to most of his pleas. The adjectival adornment attached by U.S. government agencies and the press to Soviet weapons normally varies between "advanced" and "sophisticated." Miranda speaks of MIG-21s, the same aircraft in question in 1984, described by *The Post* as "advanced," though they were first introduced in the 1950s. Even as the press invoked the whiskered MIG-21 threat, the United States sent the first two of fourteen F5E fighters to Honduras, arousing no commotion about the destabilizing effect of these mid-1970s planes on the military balance of the region.

A Militia

The thunderous verbal artillery of "massive buildup" elides the point, made by Daniel Ortega, that the prospective force of 600,000 concerns a people under arms on the Swiss model, and not a standing army, which would be inconceivable in a population of 3 million. It would have been more accurate for the Miranda stories to have been headlined "Defector Reveals Sandinistas' Plan to Reduce Regular Forces."

"Administration estimates of Cuban and Soviet military advisers in Nicaragua have been grotesquely exaggerated."

The newspapers attached something sinister to Nicaraguan hopes that the accords could be turned to advantage in eliminating the *contras* and strengthening the revolution, though ending insurgencies is what the accords are all about. That Nicaragua has contingency plans in the event of invasion distinguishes it from no other power in the world, excepting the fact that Nicaragua has actually been under attack from the mercenaries of the United States since 1981, during which time the economy has been grievously afflicted, as is evident to anyone upon arriving in Managua.

As for the Swiss bank account, according to David MacMichael of the Council on Hemispheric Affairs, the Defense Ministry does maintain such an account for the purchase of non-Soviet military equipment, which makes perfect sense given the intense U.S. pressure on European governments to deny Nicaragua arms. In any case, the U.S. contrivance of lies about imputed Sandinista complicity in drug smuggling, exposed in the Barry Seal affair and repeated by Miranda, should make one wary of any allegations of corruption.

Miranda's truly sensational disclosure is that Administration estimates of Cuban and Soviet military advisers in Nicaragua have been grotesquely exaggerated. He flatly contradicts one of Reagan's favorite rationales for the need to counter a

Soviet/Cuban "beachhead." Equally important, Miranda confirms that Nicaragua has consistently refused to supply Salvadoran rebels with surface-to-air missiles.

The most extraordinary aspect of the Administration's propaganda offensive is the obedience of the U.S. press in sticking to the government agenda and ignoring what the United States is actually doing in Nicaragua. The Guatemala accords assert that a prerequisite for peace in Central America is the termination of any form of aid "to irregular forces or insurgent movements" on the part of "regional or extraregional governments." Such aid is illegal under international law and treaty, as affirmed in June 1986 by the World Court, which condemned the United States for its actions against Nicaragua. On November 12, [1987] the U.N. General Assembly called for "full and immediate compliance" with the World Court's decision, a call opposed only by the United States and Israel, and unreported in the U.S. press.

In the three months after the accords were signed, so President Daniel Ortega reported to the Organization of American States, the C.I.A. directed 140 supply flights into Nicaragua. These were occurring as U.S. politicians and journalists were declaring that it was time to close the books on the Iran/*contra* scandal, which largely concerned illegal supply of the *contras*. *Contra* leader Adolfo Calero said Ortega's estimates were too low. In *The New York Times* for November 12, [1987], Neil Lewis tactfully altered Ortega's and Calero's reference to the supplies, terming them "surveillance flights," though the A.P. and *The Boston Globe* got it right. Just under two months earlier, on September 14, the *Los Angeles Times* reported that the C.I.A.'s flights had doubled. On October 5, [1987] the same paper informed its readers that "Western military analysts say that the contras have been stashing tons of newly airdropped weapons lately while trying to avoid heavy combat" and attacking such "soft targets" as the La Patriota farm co-op (an old woman and her 1-year-old grandson dead in predawn shelling) or villages in Rio San Juan department (six children and six adults dead). Further to display its contempt for the Guatemala accords the United States launched Operation Blazing Trail, maneuvers as big as any held in recent years in Honduran territory.

These daily breaches of law and the spirit of the accords, and the evident resolve of the C.I.A. to provision the *contras* with the means for long-term internal sabotage and destruction, ha[ve] passed entirely without censure in the mainstream U.S. press.

II

Like the ghosts of Christmas escorting Ebenezer Scrooge through Dickens's "A Christmas Carol," Maj.

Roger Miranda Bengoechea, a Nicaraguan defector, has provided a glimpse of what the future holds in store if we continue on our present course in Central America.

A Spiraling Arms Race

Major Miranda brought with him into exile the Sandinistas' five-year plan for their armed forces. With a key Congressional vote on aid to the contras coming up soon, the State Department was eager to present him to the media. In prearranged briefings, he described a Sandinista plan that calls for a continuation of the rapid military buildup that began with the contra war in 1981 and, concomitantly, a greater reliance on military aid from Cuba and the Soviet Union.

Though nothing in this plan departs significantly from Nicaragua's national security policy over the past several years, the projection of it into the 1990's conjures up a grim image of Central America caught in a spiraling arms race—each nation seeing in the weaponry of its neighbors a threat to its own security, each diverting precious resources from the tasks of economic reconstruction to preparations for war.

Preparing for Invasion

Like most military strategists, the Sandinistas have planned for the "worst case." Their projected buildup is based on the presumption that the contras, with United States assistance, will continue fighting, that Washington will remain implacably hostile and that direct United States intervention, as in Grenada, will always be possible.

In short, the Sandinistas' military plans envision exactly what the Reagan Administration is advocating: a continuation of American policy unchanged. Major Miranda has shown us the future we can expect if President Reagan gets his way.

This sobering vision of a region permanently haunted by the specter of war need not come true. The Sandinistas are not likely to carry out the military plans Major Miranda describes if the assumptions on which they are based no longer hold. Negotiations, regional and bilateral, are the only means of changing those assumptions and making the five-year plan obsolete.

Major Miranda's disclosures should make us all the more determined to press for the success of the Central American peace accord. The accord, drafted by Oscar Arias Sánchez, the Costa Rican President and 1987 Nobel Peace Prize laureate, has been implemented gradually since it was signed by five Central Americans [in August 1987]. President Arias has called on the United States not to undermine the agreement by giving more aid to the contras. . . .

That accord still offers the best hope for bringing the contra war to a political conclusion rather than having it drag on for years to a military denouement.

It also offers the best hope for stabilizing relations between Nicaragua and its neighbors.

The report of Nicaragua's planned buildup also highlights the urgency of expanding the Central American negotiations to include security issues such as the size of regional armies and the sophistication of their weaponry, and the presence of foreign military troops and advisers.

These are issues that Central Americans and the Contadora countries—Colombia, Mexico, Venezuela and Panama—wrestled with for several years before the Arias accord was signed. On several occasions, they came close to agreement only to be stymied by opposition from Washington. A security accord embodying the 1984 or 1986 Contadora proposals would explicitly prohibit the sort of Nicaraguan military buildup Major Miranda foresees.

But even a security agreement among the Central Americans is no substitute for direct talks between Nicaragua and the United States. The Sandinistas, given the history of their country, are convinced that ultimately they will have to confront American military forces directly—just as their namesake, Gen. Augusto Sandino, did in the 1920's and 30's.

So long as they harbor that expectation, they will view a large military establishment and a close relationship with Cuba and the Soviet Union as indispensable to their survival. Direct negotiations leading to a nonaggression pledge from the United States and the normalization of diplomatic and economic relations offer the only prospect of easing the Sandinistas' perception of threat. In the past, the Sandinistas have expressed a willingness to limit their armed forces in exchange for such assurances from the United States. It is time to test their sincerity.

"If the United States insists on stepping up military aid to the contras, the Soviet Union is prepared to respond in kind."

During the [1987] summit meeting, Mikhail S. Gorbachev hinted that the Soviet Union might be willing to curtail its military involvement in Nicaragua if America halted aid to the contras. His offer indicated that the Soviet Union would prefer to avoid paying for a second Cuba if there were a reasonable diplomatic alternative. On the other hand, the Nicaraguan military's five-year plan shows that if the United States insists on stepping up military aid to the contras, the Soviet Union is prepared to respond in kind.

We have before us a vision of two futures, now more clearly defined than ever before—one, peace arrived at through diplomacy; the other, a nightmare of endless war fueled by the superpowers. As with

Ebenezer Scrooge, a more enlightened sense of our self-interest can prevent our nightmare from coming true.

Alexander Cockburn is a syndicated columnist with The Nation *and* In These Times. *William M. LeoGrande is a political science professor at the American University in Washington, DC.*

viewpoint 7

The US Should Oppose the Contras

Ed Griffin-Nolan

We waved from the back of our truck as we passed a small Toyota pickup on one of the many bends along the wooded mountain road through northern Jinotega. It was noontime. The smiling man who waved back was Adrian Ferrufino, head of the local cattle ranchers and farmers union and newly appointed head of the Sandinista Front in the nearby settlement of Abisinia.

Our truck had rounded two turns and climbed a hill when the sound of gunfire and explosions stopped us. The noise came from behind us, no more than a mile or two back.

The Target of the Contras' Anger

A few minutes later I found myself kneeling on the muddy road, next to Adrian's dead body. I was talking with a wounded man who shivered in a makeshift stretcher as soldiers and local people struggled to remove the wounded and the dead, and to secure the area. Adrian's body lay side by side with that of his 24-year-old wife, Rosa Gallegos, who had been, until today, a teacher in Abisinia. Someone placed a thin sheet of plastic over their bodies to keep them dry. The rain ran off the plastic and mingled with their blood in freshly-formed puddles. Rosa's bare feet and bright-red painted toenails stuck out from beneath the plastic.

The date was June 28 [1987]. As the man on the stretcher told it, the contras had just ambushed the truck traveling behind us. Just south of a small coffee farm named La Sopresa ("The Surprise"), not quite 100 miles from Managua, 10 or 15 armed men hid in the bushes, patiently waited as we passed through their gun-sights, then opened fire on Adrian, Rosa, and half-a-dozen other passengers. Four people jumped to safety, scraped but untouched by the bullets. The wounded man, a member of a local

militia unit, was shot in the leg as he attempted to fire back at the attackers.

A 60-year-old woman known only as "the one who sells bread," wasn't as lucky. Shrapnel gouged a hole in her temple and she was thrown from the truck as it dove off into a ravine. It slammed into a tree 50 feet down, and threw the woman clear, breaking her jaw and two collarbones, fracturing her skull, and destroying one eye. Seeing her slung in a hammock stretcher lashed to the back of an ancient Chevy pickup, I thought of the three hours of bumpy roads between her and the nearest hospital. My only prayer was for a quick and merciful death—there seemed no way she could survive.

While in one sense we were very close to death ourselves, in another sense we could have been a million miles away. Adrian was the target of the contras' anger. His face, his truck, and his work were well known in the area. Everyone we talked to believed the contras were gunning for him.

The Price of "Pressure"

His was dangerous work. His predecessor, Fran Gutierrez, was still hospitalized with a head wound from an earlier ambush. Since that time, we have heard that Fran returned from the hospital and was killed in late August [1987] in yet another ambush.

"We" were a group of Witness for Peace investigators accompanied by two journalists. Our purpose in traveling in northern Nicaragua was to interview survivors and gather evidence about contra attacks like this one.

The contras target rural community leaders and people who work in rural development, health, education, and social projects. People like Adrian Ferrufino who work with the government and with agrarian reform. People like Rosa Gallegos, who teach school. Like Manuel Lopez Ibanez, a Chilean exile and agronomist who was dragged from his truck, beaten and shot to death on June 24 [1987].

Ed Griffin-Nolan, "Trailing the Contras," *Christianity & Crisis*, October 26, 1987. Reprinted with permission. Copyright 1987, Christianity & Crisis, 537 West 121st St., New York, New York 10027.

Construction workers, engineers like Benjamin Linder, lumber workers, drivers—the contras have continued to target and kill such people.

The contras view people like Adrian and Rosa as spreaders of an alien ideology, usurpers of power, and squatters on their land. Killing people like them is part of what the Reagan administration terms "putting pressure" on the Nicaraguan government.

When the bodies were driven away and the wounded were en route to a hospital, we drove back to Abisinia to talk to the survivors. They did not speak of geopolitical considerations and did not seem concerned about alien ideologies.

"The contras are killing off the best and the brightest of a generation of young and service-oriented Nicaraguans."

"He was the one who pulled out all the nails here," one man told us, when asked to describe what Adrian meant to the people in Abisinia. The man was using an old and uniquely Nicaraguan phrase which is shorthand for problem solving. "He was the one who was helping resolve the social problems here. His truck was really well known . . . taking people back and forth, bringing in materials, looking out for the well-being of the community." Rosa Gallegos' death meant one less teacher in an area where, according to Rigoberto Medrano, a survivor of the ambush who works with the Education Ministry, "we have already had to close four adult education centers because they [the contras] kidnap the teachers."

Killing the Best and Brightest

In ambushes like this one, and in selective assassinations, the contras are killing off the best and the brightest of a generation of young and service-oriented Nicaraguans. This has been their pattern in the past, and it seems to have only intensified in the period when significant numbers of contra units, with newly U.S.-trained field commanders, infiltrated back into Nicaragua after nearly two years in their Honduran bases.

Health *brigadistas*—volunteer workers trained in preventive medicine—are another high-risk group. "Before the war," says Maria Felitza, the doctor in El Cua, Jinotega, "one could go off into the mountains for days to vaccinate. After the war started that became suicide. To be a brigadista was an honor; now it is a heroic act." Maria Felitza moved to El Cua after a good friend, Ambrosio Mogorron, was killed when a mine blew up the truck in which he was traveling with eight other members of a vaccination team last May [1987]. Attacks against health workers impact coming generations as well—

in many areas of the north, children are dying from diseases which, in the early years of the Revolution, were essentially eradicated.

Another contra tendency—some would say obsession—is toward attacking agricultural cooperatives. Witness for Peace investigated 19 attacks against cooperatives in which at least 84 civilians were killed or wounded. These cooperative farms are typically defended by the local people who live on and work the land. They grow coffee, corn, beans, and some of them raise cattle and other livestock. They range in size from two houses to as many as 40. The contras and their supporters who attack Witness for Peace and others who have reported this pattern claim that the cooperatives are really military bases in which the Sandinistas hide behind the civilian populations as a shield.

The cooperatives are not military bases. One of the farms attacked was a completely undefended community of evangelical Protestants who refused to bear arms as a matter of religious conviction. Fourteen of them were defended by the militia, and in the four cases where there were any army troops present, they were few in number. The contras have at times attacked cooperatives where the army sometimes stays, but have been careful to hit on nights when the army is elsewhere (in this respect the contras have been greatly assisted by intelligence reports provided by the U.S.).

Many residents of the cooperatives are people who have fled from their homes deeper in the mountains because of the war. Some have been through three or even four contra attacks already. In a typical attack, the contras open fire on the houses where the people are asleep and the other farm buildings, even though the defenders are usually in the trenches in the surrounding hills. When the defenders are killed or have retreated, the contras then move into the community and burn the houses, killing or kidnaping civilians if they have not fled.

The Contras' Intentions

In several cases, survivors report contra commanders told them they would be attacked again if they did not leave the cooperatives and move to private farms. In another attack on Abisinia, a contra leader by the name of Danilo, after burning down the people's houses, told them that if they rebuilt their houses 100 times, he and his men would return to burn them down 100 times. It is interesting to note that he did not say that he would attack if they had an army presence or if they had a militia. He said that if they rebuilt their homes, their homes would be burnt down. This seems to be a much clearer statement of the contras' intent than we are likely to hear from any of the well-dressed contra leaders parading about Washington or press-conferencing in Miami.

One final note. Clarisa Altimirano, the bread lady

caught in the June 28 ambush, survived. One of the long-term Witness for Peace volunteers, Julieta Martinez, found her in the Jinotega hospital a week later. She was badly hurt, but doctors believe she will live. Finding her was a joyful surprise for all of us. The signing of the Central American peace plan by the five presidents on August 7 [1987] was another such surprise, miracle, moment of grace, call it what you will. It is no exaggeration to say that it has changed everything in Central America.

"The road to peace is not going to be short or easy."

The peace plan, and the National Reconciliation Commission now established in Nicaragua in compliance with the plan, have not brought an end to the war. Indeed, since the signing of the pact, the contras have assassinated at least two people who were traveling on missions to speak to rural families about the amnesty law for contras who turn in their arms. The road to peace is not going to be short or easy.

The Choice Is Clear

But the choice that the U.S. faces is now quite clear—either accept the will of the Central American presidents and endorse the Guatemala agreements, or vote more of our money for ambushes, assassinations, kidnaping, and worse by the contras. The administration can no longer credibly argue that the contras are freedom fighters and that their human rights abuses are tangential. In the wake of the Guatemala accords, Congress can no longer complain that they have no alternative program.

Ed Griffin-Nolan is a researcher and writer with Witness for Peace, an organization that sends Americans to visit combat areas in Nicaragua.

"The enslavement of Nicaragua is one step closer to the enslavement of the world."

The US Should Oppose the Sandinistas

Jesse Helms

Is Nicaragua a Communist country? Some refuse to concede that it is. Even some religious leaders—those who should be particularly alert to the Godless, atheistic purpose of Communist rule—profess to defend the Marxist Sandinista regime in Managua. They declare that the present dictatorship has created a more just society than the previous Government of Anastasio Somoza. They assert that the Communist rulers are much closer to "the people" and are more deeply dedicated to their welfare.

Many of these people are simply misled. They don't know what happened in Nicaragua in the past. They don't know what is happening today. . . .

Somoza Shoved Out

The notion that the 1979 Sandinista takeover was a democratic revolution is totally false. As soon as Castro saw in 1978 that the United States had given away the Panama Canal—thereby setting in motion a scenario for U.S. withdrawal from the region—he called the Sandinista leaders to Havana and read them the riot act. He told them that it was not enough to be Marxist-Leninists; they had to be disciplined as well. And he, Castro, was going to apply the discipline.

Under the Castro plan, the Sandinista factions would give up their quarrels and adopt a united front with the non-Communist enemies of Somoza. Under those conditions Castro would finance them and provide them with arms through the dictator of Panama, Omar Torrijos, and Torrijos's chief henchman, Manuel Noriega. The United States was fully aware of this meeting, as proved by C.I.A. documents that were later published in the *Congressional Record.*

But not all the weapons came from Castro. Plenty of weapons came from the United States, illegally shipped with the collusion of the Carter Administration to a certain "Panamanian Sportsmen's Club" run by Colonel Noriega. Congressional hearings on Capitol Hill viewed and examined weapons captured by [Anastasio] Somoza which had been sent to Noriega from Miami with U.S. Government collusion.

In July of 1979, the U.S. State Department played a pivotal role in forcing Somoza to leave Nicaragua for exile in Paraguay, where he was later assassinated by a Sandinista hit squad. Somoza's National Guard was not so much defeated as demoralized by Carter policy. Key State Department officials welcomed the Sandinistas into Managua, another in the series of Communist "Liberators" championed everywhere by U.S. diplomats. . . .

Meanwhile, the Cubans and the Soviets began exercising their muscle. As early as July 20, 1979, Brezhnev expressed Soviet willingness "to develop multifaceted ties with Nicaragua." In March 1980, the first major Nicaraguan delegation arrived in Moscow and signed a party-to-party mutual support agreement between the Soviet Communist Party and the Sandinistas, a pact far more significant than if it had been a lower-level agreement between the two countries. In Communist countries the state is a bourgeois facade destined to wither away; the party is king. Such agreements are made only with countries that Moscow considers to be firmly within the Communist bloc. The top Sandinista leaders followed this up with a remarkable number of trips to Moscow between May 1982 and mid-1983.

Allied with Communists

Whereas the United States sent foreign aid, the Soviets sent credits redeemable only for Soviet goods. There is no doubt whatsoever that Nicaragua is part of the Soviet bloc. It has associate member status in CEMA, the Soviet bloc economic

Jesse Helms, "Why We Must Act To Help Nicaragua," *Conservative Digest,* September 1987. Reprinted with permission.

community, and CEMA has held its annual meeting in Managua. From the beginning, the Soviets made available $50 million in credits, Libya $100 million, and $64 million came from Cuba. In 1982, the Soviets offered another $150 million in credits. By the end of 1985, Soviet bloc countries had contributed a total of $1.04 billion.

None of this went to help the Nicaraguan people. Instead, Nicaragua staged the most massive military buildup ever seen in Latin America. From a guerrilla force of 5,000, the Sandinista army grew to 16,625 by December 1979, and to 23,750 by 1982. Nicaragua now has an active-duty force of over 75,000 with about 60,000 more in the reserves and the militia.

This may be compared with Somoza's National Guard, which never numbered more than 14,000. Next door Honduras has 22,000 troops, and neighboring Costa Rica has none.

"Cuban support for the Sandinistas has been extensive from the beginning."

Indeed, Nicaragua has more armored vehicles, artillery, and air-defense weapons than all other Central American countries combined. From 1979 to 1985, the Sandinistas received at least $1.2 billion in military assistance from Cuba and the Soviet bloc. Since 1981, they have received 79,600 tons of equipment. Last year alone the Soviets sent 23,000 tons, valued at $600 million.

Cuban support for the Sandinistas has been extensive from the beginning. Cuban Communists organized the Sandinista political system, and Cuban advisors act at all military levels, even playing an operational role. There are now over 65,000 Cubans in Nicaragua, including military and intelligence advisors, and civilian technicians such as those now building the military airports.

Loss of Freedom

More insidious than the military presence is the Cuban program of indoctrination. The Communists know that "the people" will never accept the doctrines of Communism until a whole generation or more of children has been trained in an education that systematically excludes the truth. In 1979, the first thing the Cubans did was to send thousands of teachers trained in Communist indoctrination to replace teachers loyal to Judeo-Christian precepts and to Western civilization.

Since 1980, more than 3,000 Nicaraguan students have been sent to Cuba for secondary, undergraduate, and graduate training. In 1986, a new program was started with 350 children between the ages of twelve and sixteen sent to Cuba for six

years. They will not be allowed to return for visits or to see their parents until their political indoctrination is completed. Eventually, these children will form the hard-core elite for the new masters of Nicaragua.

Meanwhile, all children in Nicaragua are subjected to a constant flow of Soviet propaganda. East Germany has sent 4.7 million school textbooks in Spanish. The Sandinista newspapers are full of tributes to the Soviet system, and so are the state-run TV and feature films.

In 1982 the Sandinista regime officially suspended most civil rights. In 1984 it was announced that some rights were being restored in preparation for elections which were to be forthcoming. But it soon became evident that there would be no free elections in Nicaragua. Opponents were denied the right to organize freely, to debate issues, to obtain TV time. One by one the major candidates withdrew because of the farce. By 1985 the Sandinistas formalized what had in fact already taken place. On October 15th of that year, all the fundamental civil-rights guarantees that had been announced on August 31, 1979, were formally suspended.

Dictatorship

On January 9, 1987, Nicaragua promulgated its new Constitution. But three hours later the Sandinistas further announced that the following rights guaranteed in that Constitution would be suspended:

• Right of personal freedom, personal security, and *habeas corpus*;
• Right to be presumed innocent until proven guilty;
• Right to trial and appeal;
• Freedom of movement;
• Freedom from arbitrary interference in personal life, family, home, and correspondence;
• Freedom of information;
• Freedom of expression;
• Right of peaceful assembly;
• Freedom of association;
• Right to organize unions;
• Right to strike.

It is not surprising, then, that there are between 8,000 and 10,000 political prisoners in Sandinista jails where they have suffered abuse and torture. (Somoza's political prisoners never numbered more than a few hundred.) Human-rights organizations report at least 32 political killings [in 1986] by the Sandinistas, and 20 prisoners killed; as many as 500 civilians have been killed by the Sandinista military. There were mass arrests of 5,300 civilians in 1986. According to the Sandinistas' own statistics, over 200,000 rural residents were forcibly relocated.

Nor did this violence occur at random. There has been a systematic stifling of the opposition. *La Prensa*, the last surviving opposition paper, was closed. Radio Catolica, the last opposition radio station, was closed. Leaders of surviving opposition political parties were targeted for abuse, threats, legal harassment, and expulsion.

Finally, as in Poland, opposition left the political level and began to center in the churches. The Sandinistas did not dare to attack Archbishop Miguel Obando y Bravo, a man from a country background and deeply beloved by the people; instead they expelled his chief assistant, Bishop Pablo Antonio Vega. . . .

Fight for Freedom

Can the house stand if it is half-slave and half-free? Can the world survive in freedom if we do not support those who are willing to fight and die for freedom? Will we retain our own freedom in the United States if we no longer think that freedom is worth fighting for? The enslavement of Nicaragua is one step closer to the enslavement of the world, but it is a step right in our own hemisphere, and on our very own continent. If we fail to help the freedom fighters, we fail to help ourselves.

Jesse Helms is a Republican US senator from North Carolina.

"The media will not expose what they know to be true, and Congress will not constrain the terrorist commanders as long as they seem to be succeeding in their tasks."

viewpoint 9

The Media Misrepresent the Sandinistas in a Negative Light

Noam Chomsky

On August 7, 1987, the Central American Presidents signed a peace agreement in Guatemala City [the Arias plan] which, if implemented, could have a significant impact in the region. The agreement does not address the causes of the violence and suffering that plague these long-term U.S. dependencies, but it might restrict U.S. intervention, a prerequisite to any constructive change. The circumstances of the accords should be carefully studied by those who hope to influence state policy, but I will defer this crucial topic, keeping here to the prospects for implementation of the accords.

In approaching this question, we must bear in mind that we live in the Age of Orwell, in which every term has two meanings: its literal meaning, largely irrelevant in practice, and the operative meaning, devised in the interests of established power. Accordingly, there are two versions of the accords to consider: the actual text, and the radically different Washington version. . . .

The Irrelevant Facts

Keeping to the actual substance of the accords, there is no possibility that they can be implemented, as a review of the initial three-month period clearly demonstrates.

The accords identify one factor as "an indispensable element to achieving a stable and lasting peace in the region," namely, termination of any form of aid "to irregular forces or insurgent movements" on the part of "regional or extra-regional" governments. As a corollary, the Central American governments agree to deny their territory to any such groups. This demand is directed at the United States and the client states it has used for the attack against Nicaragua by what contra lobbyists

candidly describe in internal documents as a "proxy force," organized, trained, supplied and controlled by the CIA.

This central feature of the accords is redundant, since such actions are barred by a higher authority: by international law and treaty, hence by the supreme law of the land under the U.S. Constitution. . . . The fact was underscored by the World Court in June 1986 as it condemned the United States for its "unlawful use of force" against Nicaragua and called upon it to desist from these crimes. Congress responded by voting $100 million of aid and freeing the CIA to direct the attack and to use its own funds on an unknown scale. The U.S. vetoed a UN Security Council resolution calling on all states to observe international law and voted against a General Assembly resolution to the same effect, joined by Israel and El Salvador. On November 12, 1987, the General Assembly again called for "full and immediate compliance" with the World Court decision. This time only Israel joined with the U.S. in opposing adherence to international law, another blow to the Central American accords, unreported by the national press as usual.

The media had dismissed the World Court as a "hostile forum" whose decisions are irrelevant, while liberal advocates of world order explained that the U.S. must disregard the Court decision. With this reaction, U.S. elites clearly articulate their self-image: the United States is a lawless terrorist state, which stands above the law and is entitled to undertake violence, as it chooses, in support of its objectives. The reaction to the "indispensable element" of the Central American accords merely reiterated that conviction.

To ensure that the accords would be undermined, the U.S. at once directed its proxy forces to escalate military actions, also increasing the regular supply flights that are required to keep them in the field. These had passed the level of one a day in the

Excerpted from "Is Peace at Hand?" by Noam Chomsky in the January 1988 issue of *Zeta* magazine. Reprinted with the author's permission.

preceding months in support of the "spring offensive," designed to achieve sufficient levels of terror and disruption to impress Congress. The proxy army followed Washington's orders to attack "soft targets" such as farm cooperatives and health clinics instead of "trying to duke it out with the Sandinistas directly," as explained by General John Galvin, commander of the U.S. Southern Command, who added that with these tactics, aimed at civilians lacking means of defense against armed terrorist bands, prospects for the contras should improve. The State Department officially authorized such attacks, with the support of media doves. There are other terrorist states, but to my knowledge, the United States is alone today in *officially* endorsing international terrorism. We see here another illustration of the self-image of U.S. elites: in a terrorist culture, all that counts is the success of violence. Accordingly, debate in Congress and the media focused on the question of whether the violence could succeed, with "doves" arguing that the proxy army was inept and hawks replying that it must be given more time and aid to prove itself as a successful terrorist force—putting euphemisms aside.

Distorting the Accords

Undersecretary of State Elliott Abrams conducted a news conference by radio in the Central American capitals on October 22 [1987], unreported in the national press, at which he announced that the United States will "never accept a Soviet satellite in Central America"—meaning a country that is not a loyal U.S. satellite—and that "We're going to continue the aid to the resistance," to be sure, in violation of the "indispensable element" for peace. The Reagan administration announced its intention to seek congressional backing for its war, and Congress obliged by providing "humanitarian" aid—meaning, any form of aid that the government chooses to send—in direct violation of the accords. Secretary of State George Shultz informed the OAS [Organization of American States] that the U.S. would persist in the unlawful use of force by its "resistance fighters" until a "free Nicaragua" is established by Washington standards, thus consigning the accords to oblivion, along with international law. This announcement was noted in a 140-word item in the *Times* stressing Washington's intent to give the accords "every chance," while a headline in the liberal *Boston Globe* reported approvingly that the U.S. is "easing [its] stance."

While the media and Congress took note of Washington's plans for the future, the actual steps taken to undermine the central elements of the peace agreements passed in virtual silence, in accord with the principle that the United States is entitled to employ violence as it chooses. The same basic principle explains the elite consensus, including the most outspoken doves, that Nicaragua must not be

permitted to obtain aircraft to defend its territory. The pretense of liberal Congresspeople and others that such aircraft would be a threat to the United States may be dismissed with no comment. The real intent is obvious: the terrorist superpower must be free to penetrate Nicaraguan airspace at will for surveillance and coordination of the attacks on "soft targets" by its proxy forces, and to provide them with arms and supplies.

Washington Fiction

These crucial facts suffice to demonstrate that in terms of their irrelevant substance, the accords were dead before the ink was dry, with the full support of congressional liberals and elite opinion generally.

Note that as tacitly conceded on all sides, the proxy forces bear no resemblance to guerrillas. Rather, they are, by the standards of the region, a well-equipped mercenary army maintained by overwhelming U.S. power; their supporters insist that they would collapse if this unlawful aid and control were to be withdrawn. The contrast to authentic guerrillas, as in El Salvador, is dramatic, but suppressed, in the interest of maintaining the Washington fiction of a "symmetry" between Nicaragua and El Salvador. There is indeed a symmetry, though not the one put forth by Washington and its Free Press. In both countries, there is a terrorist army attacking "soft targets" and slaughtering civilians, and in both countries, it is organized and maintained by the United States: the army of El Salvador, and the proxy army attacking Nicaragua from foreign bases. The symmetry reaches to fine details. In El Salvador too, the U.S. mercenary forces attack cooperatives, killing, raping and abducting members, as Americas Watch has reported. . . .

"The actual steps taken to undermine the central elements of the [Arias] peace agreements passed in virtual silence."

From the first days after the accords were signed, the media assured us that whatever may appear in the irrelevant text, "there is no doubt that [the treaty's] main provisions are principally directed at Nicaragua and will affect Nicaragua more than any of the other nations that signed the accord"—which is certainly true, under the conditions of obedience dictated by Washington, though this was presumably not the point intended by James LeMoyne [*New York Times* Central America correspondent]. As he explained further, the Sandinistas are "in a somewhat exposed position" because they, and they alone, "are under close scrutiny for their efforts to carry out the Central American peace treaty"—as dictated by Washington, whose orders are naturally binding. *Times* correspondent Stephen Kinzer informed us that the peace accord "requires Nicaragua to permit full press and political freedom" while requiring "other countries in the region to stop supporting" the contras; a half-truth that amounts to a lie, since the accord also requires the other states to permit full press and political freedom, which is inconceivable as long as the security forces are not dismantled and the U.S. remains in command.

"It would be an error to describe such media subservience as totalitarianism in the Stalinist or Nazi style. . . . Here we see, rather, a form of voluntary servitude."

I do not mean to suggest that Kinzer is incapable of outright falsehoods; for example, his statement in the same column that the Nicaraguan government refused to allow the "Roman Catholic radio station to broadcast news." This is one of his favorite tales, repeated in several other columns and by LeMoyne as well, along with the claim that the Ministry of Interior refused to comment on the matter (October 20 [1987]). AP [Associated Press] reported the same day the statement of the Interior Ministry that "Radio Catolica may broadcast news, but must apply for the legally required permission for the program and register the name of its director, the broadcast time and other information"—not exactly a decisive proof that this is a totalitarian dungeon. . . .

The Operative Illusions

According to the U.S. version, the sole question is whether the accords will be implemented by Nicaragua—according to the standards set by Washington. These standards were readily predictable from the start. Since Washington is determined to undermine the agreements, any respect in which Nicaragua adheres to them is off the agenda. We are permitted to discuss some element of the accords only if Washington's interpretation differs from Nicaragua's, so that Nicaragua is in violation—by definition. The task of the media, then, is to conduct a parody of the sciences. In the sciences, one confronts some puzzling facts and attempts to devise principles that will explain them. In ideological warfare, one begins with Higher Truths dictated from above. The task is to select the facts, or to invent them, in such a way as to render the required conclusions not too transparently absurd—at least for properly disciplined minds. . . .

It would be an error to describe such media subservience as totalitarianism in the Stalinist or Nazi style. In totalitarian states, those who serve power have the excuse of fear. Here we see, rather, a form of voluntary servitude, a remarkable and pervasive feature of the intellectual culture.

For its first commentary on the initial three-month phase of the accords, the *Times* selected James Chace, a noted dove. Accordingly, he expressed pleasure with the progress on all fronts, even Nicaragua, where President Ortega "has agreed to negotiate indirectly with the contras," thus indicating that at last "the Sandinistas seem determined to fulfill the main provisions" of the agreement, as defined by Washington. But "there is still, of course, a long way to go" in consummating the accords, because "the Sandinistas have not yet declared a general amnesty or lifted the state of emergency." Apart from continued Sandinista obstruction, Chace sees no problems during the three-month period, though as a dove, he opposes renewed contra aid and criticizes the Reagan administration for remaining "suspicious and hostile," while conceding that it has good grounds, since "the Guatemala agreement does not provide for reductions in Soviet aid to Managua" so that "America's legitimate security concerns" are not addressed. Among the topics unmentioned are: U.S. actions to undermine the accords; the violation of their essential provisions by the U.S. client states; the fact that "Soviet aid to Managua" was a major achievement of the Reagan administration, which blocked aid from elsewhere while launching an attack on Nicaragua, and that the Guatemala agreement also does not provide for reductions in U.S. aid to its client states; that others, besides the beleaguered and helpless United States, have "legitimate security concerns," among them Nicaragua and the victims of U.S. aid in the terror states; that Managua has long offered to exclude foreign advisers and negotiate verifiable security guarantees, efforts successfully blocked by Washington; that if Nicaragua poses "security concerns" for the United States, then Luxembourg poses security concerns for the Soviet Union, and Denmark, a member of a hostile military alliance, poses far greater concerns, so that the USSR is entitled, by our principles, to organize terrorist forces to attack and overthrow their governments unless they agree to disarm and offer verifiable guarantees that they will no longer threaten the Soviet Union. . . .

No Serious Discussion

The attack against Nicaragua and the programs of state terror to suppress democracy and social reform in the client states reflect an elite consensus. That is why they are not discussed in any minimally serious way. The media will not expose what they know to be true, and Congress will not constrain the terrorist commanders as long as they seem to be succeeding in their tasks. The fate of the Central American accords lies in the hands of the domestic enemy of the state, the citizens in "enemy territory" at home. As so often in the past, dissent, protest, pressures of a wide variety that escape elite control can modify the calculus of costs of planners, and offer a slight hope that Washington can be compelled to permit at least some steps towards "justice, freedom and democracy" within its domains.

Noam Chomsky is a professor at the Massachusetts Institute of Technology who writes often about the US and Central America.

"Beware, then, reports issued by groups . . . filled with selective perceptions of the political scene or so-called abuses by the contra rebels."

viewpoint **10**

The Media Misrepresent the Sandinistas in a Positive Light

David Brock

The first week of November [1987] was a big one for world Communism, as Messrs. Gorbachev, Honecker, Jaruzelski, and Castro gathered atop Lenin's tomb in Red Square to celebrate the 70th anniversary of the revolution that brought the Bolsheviks to power, and Nicaraguan strongman Daniel Ortega, with not inconsiderable energy, set about consolidating his. Ortega, of course, is not so firmly ensconced as his eminent mentors; his position, in fact, was so precarious that the Comandante de la Revolucion was compelled to leave his comrades in Moscow two days before the climactic event, the November 7 parade of tanks and missiles, to deliver a speech on peace in Managua that he would later call a watershed in his political career.

That Ortega's prospects are contingent more on the vagaries of international opinion than on the popular support of Nicaraguans has long been a testament to the inherent weakness of his Marxist-Leninist project. Ortega's gambit was to announce concessions that would have a niggling effect on his hegemony at home but a titanic resonance on the world scene, generating enough momentum to Contadoraize the peace plan of Costa Rican President Oscar Arias. So when he ascended a wooden platform at dusk to exhort a throng of 30,000 Sandinistas in Revolution Plaza, the stage had been painstakingly choreographed for external consumption.

Media Supporting Sandinistas

About 200 foreign reporters had been given credentials by the government's Interpren office to cover the event, paying $35 each in their national currency. (With inflation at 1,000 percent, the government won't accept its own cordoba.) A "mass rally" had been convened, though most all of those gathered were Sandinista Popular Army soldiers, appearing very much the wild-eyed, grisly guerrillas of Sandinista lore. Several of those not in uniform wore T-shirts with the internationalist epigram: "Aquino is not the answer. Solidarity with the New People's Army."

The press stood on a platform directly in front of, but somewhat below, Ortega's. Several dozen Sandinistas coached to display revolutionary euphoria—including most of the women in the crowd—surrounded the press, waving red and black Sandinista National Liberation Front [FSLN] flags and running frenzied circles around one another. The press was gently nudged by Comandante Tomas Borge's secret police (officially "the sentinels of the people's happiness") to photograph this unrepresentative spectacle and record their chant: "Fight against the Yanqui, enemy of all humanity." The rest of the crowd was far less engaged in the matter at hand; they made human pyramids, smoked marijuana, and began trailing off soon after Ortega started speaking.

But these pyrotechnics of peace were after all of marginal import. For the most obvious and distressing revelation on a Nicaraguan tour—more than what Nicaraguans call *la razzia*, the ravaging of bodies, minds, and spirits that the Sandinista revolution has wrought, more even than the extent of the toilet paper shortage—is that most foreign visitors here need none of Ortega's petulant preaching. They are already converted to his cause.

Arriving at the air-conditioned offices of Interpren, where the foreign press corps had gathered for an appropriate snack of animal crackers and cherry soda before being taken to hear Ortega, one instantly spotted the *de rigueur* attire for covering an FSLN rally: red and black. More than one quarter of the press had chosen to express its support for the

David Brock, "Danny Ortega's American Janissaries," *The American Spectator,* January 1988. Reprinted with permission.

Sandinistas in this fashion. There was the rotund Canadian television reporter in a red and black polo shirt and the svelte Australian magazine writer in a red jumpsuit and black tank-top. Others donned simple red and black wrist bands.

Anti-Contra Bias

Bias is one of the few abundant commodities in Managua, though among Americans it manifests itself in more politically acceptable anti-contra, rather than pro-Sandinista, sentiments. Lucy Siegel, a reporter for CBS News, told me flat out: "Personally, I think the contras are worthless." The CBS Managua bureau is not known for subtlety; the bureau producer, Courtney "Cookie" Hood, has acknowledged entertaining Borge, the interior minister, in the hotel room where she resides. And such unseemliness is not the sole province of CBS: Rod Nordland, the author of a highly critical *Newsweek* story on the contras in June[1987], was keeping house at the time with a woman reporter for *Barricada,* the official FSLN daily. Gone, one supposes, are the good old days of adversarial reporting so dutifully practiced when Anastasio Somoza ruled.

On November 4 [1987], the night before the Arias plan's deadline, ABC's Richard Threlkeld filed a breathlessly enthusiastic story on steps already undertaken by the Sandinistas to comply with the plan, even though only the reopening of the opposition newspaper *La Prensa* could qualify as a positive move. The *New York Times*'s Stephen Kinzer put the best face possible on Ortega's speech the next day, describing his proposal to negotiate a technical cease-fire as a "dramatic reversal." Ortega, though, had not moved a bit from the slogans on FSLN banners that had festooned the city days before: "Political Dialogue: Never! Never! Never!" and "No General Amnesty." Readers of Kinzer's report would not know that Ortega had also rescinded the government's declared cease-fire, giving the contras 48 hours to lay down their arms or "we are going to go after them with sticks and lead," or that he had reactivated the *turbas divinas,* thugs paid by the government to harass the internal political opposition.

The next night, NBC aired a report on Ortega's invitation to Miguel Cardinal Obando y Bravo to mediate the cease-fire talks. Ramiro Gurdian, identified as "one of Ortega's most uncompromising critics," was shown praising this "positive step." The next morning Gurdian told me: "That's the trouble with the foreign press. I said it was a positive step, but that the Sandinistas had not complied with any of the other parts of the plan. The second part got cut."

Disillusioned with the Soviet Union, China, Vietnam, and maybe even Cuba, foreign correspondents and political pilgrims the world over

now head to Managua, clad in the latest camouflage gear from Banana Republic, in the hope of finding a genuinely liberating people's revolution, a nation searching for self-determination and social justice. In a wicker-laden lobby of the famed Intercontinental Hotel, known as the media bazaar, one might spot Warren Beatty or Richard Gere being escorted by a free-lance tour guide like Dr. Charles Clements, chairman of Pax Americas, a pro-Sandinista lobby. (Clements also identifies himself as a consultant to Rep. David Bonior, the Michigan Democrat who has received $5,000 in campaign contributions from Pax Americas.) Such tours are carefully coordinated with the government to show what it wants seen: model cooperatives, model schools, and model hospitals as well as sites of alleged contra atrocities. Not on the schedule are local supermarkets where people wait all day to scan nearly bare shelves, or the underground solitary confinement prisons that house 10,000 political dissenters, or the burned-out villages of Miskito Indians.

> *"Foreign correspondents and political pilgrims the world over now head to Managua . . . in the hope of finding a genuinely liberating people's revolution."*

Borge, the Sandinista disinformation wizard, receives journalists in a modest house used only for this purpose and religious delegations in a special office adorned with crucifixes. He approves the itineraries of foreign visitors so that he may dispatch police to neighborhoods on the agenda to lock up "potential enemies" and form "casual encounter teams"—police posing as content local residents. Despite this, most visitors get a dose of reality when they see the massive hard-currency mall and elaborate nightclubs frequented by Sandinista officials, as well as their lush residential suburb, reached by driving past ten miles of the shabbiest housing one is likely to see in Latin America; but they politely choose not to talk about it. Nor do they seem to want to talk about the few bookstores in Managua, all of which display large portraits of Marx, Lenin, Castro, and Qaddafi and offer no books published outside the Communist bloc. And what are they to make of the large contingent of Russians, East Germans, Bulgarians, Cubans, and Libyans one is likely to encounter shuffling through government offices and hotels?

This week in November [1987] neither Gere nor Beatty was to be found. The only hunk in town was New York Mayor Ed Koch. Hizzoner was leading a tour of nine New Yorkers, and they seemed to do a better job than most of getting past the government's staged events. Koch met with Violetta Chamorro, the editor of *La Prensa*, and held a press conference with anti-Sandinista activists of the Democratic Coordinating Committee. (Political parties are not allowed to function otherwise, but they may hold press conferences.) Later in the day, after what must have been a metaphysical encounter with Ortega, Koch hailed him as a "brilliant leader who will find peace in an expeditious way. . . . Am I more supportive of them than before I came here? The answer is yes. I will be softer, as it relates to my criticism."

Ignoring the Evidence

Beware, then, reports issued by groups like Koch's filled with selective perceptions of the political scene or so-called abuses by the contra rebels. In the end, Koch turned out to be like most fact-finders here, favorably disposed to the Sandinistas at the outset (he threw a cocktail party for Ortega in New York after the 1979 revolution) and even more exuberant, despite ghastly contrary evidence, upon departure. Also in this category falls Sen. Christopher Dodd, in town as, inexplicably, the chairman of the Senate's Central American Negotiations Observer Group. Dodd, as well as scores of foreign aid officials from so-called neutralist countries like the Netherlands, Sweden, and Switzerland, have descended upon Managua, frantically advising Ortega on the minimum steps he must take to remain in their good graces. They are easily pleased. (William LeoGrande, the oft-quoted Latinist of American University, was overheard at poolside at the Intercontinental, advising the comandantes to stall through negotiations until Reagan leaves office. Then, with a Democrat in the White House, "you can do anything you want.")

Another large contingent of visitors in Nicaragua does not attempt to create the semblance of objectivity. They come under the sponsorship of groups like Witness for Peace, formed in 1983 with the explicit endorsement of Borge, and spend up to three weeks teaching in schools, working on state-owned farms harvesting coffee and sugar cane, painting revolutionary murals on the sides of buildings, and holding vigils alongside Sandinista soldiers to repel contra attacks. An estimated 100,000 Americans have taken such political tours of Nicaragua, and thousands more have come in international labor brigades from Canada, Sweden, Finland, West Germany, and Spain. Though production here is less than three-quarters what it was in 1978, these well-heeled volunteers, paying up to $2,000 each to make the trip, enable the economy to limp along, replacing the young men who have been drafted in unprecedented numbers into a Sandinista army that is larger than the armies of all the other Central American nations combined.

The Nicaragua Exchange—the source of the "come join the harvest" ads in the *Nation*—has sent about 3,000 Americans to Nicaragua. Upon returning, they are asked to "please get your story, whatever it may be, into the papers, on the radio, on TV." The Exchange also tells them how to raise tax-deductible . . . contributions for the Sandinistas from their friends. A group called Quest for Peace has already raised $50 million in aid that inevitably is put to military use.

Americans Fighting with Sandinistas

The Americans are a particular source of pride for the Sandinistas, allowing them to argue that only Ronald Reagan, not the U.S. public, has a beef with them. In addition, the comandantes are said to be convinced that the U.S. would not contemplate pulling a Grenada in Nicaragua so long as there are so many Americans here—from 1,000 to 2,000 at any given moment. The Americans also are used to undermine U.S. foreign policy more directly. Sandinista cooperatives, which attract many American volunteers, serve a dual purpose: many members are armed and receive military training, making them legitimate targets for the contras. But when an American is killed—as was Benjamin Linder, himself armed with a Soviet AK-47 rifle, last spring—the Sandinistas cynically turn it into a propaganda coup.

Linder was one of a growing number of "sandalistas," Americans who go to Nicaragua not to visit, but to live and work and even fight. The upper echelons of the Sandinista Front are full of such people—Miguel d'Escoto, the foreign minister; Paul Atha, a special assistant to Borge; Robert Vargas of the Sandinista Department of Agitation and Propaganda; and scores of Maryknoll nuns. These expatriates, who understand well the American political system, are engaged in an international campaign of deception to choke off supplies to the contras and to ensure peace—on Sandinista terms.

"These expatriates, who understand well the American political system, are engaged in an international campaign of deception to choke off supplies to the contras and to ensure peace—on Sandinista terms."

On the plane from Miami to Managua, a student from the University of Oregon told me he was about to spend a few weeks in Nicaragua working for the Sandinistas as part of a class project. He had been there a year ago, on a Witness for Peace tour, and assured me I would be amazed to see the new Nicaragua. And amazed I was, at the wide chasm between this American's stunning misapprehension of Sandinista Nicaragua and the feelings of every Nicaraguan I talked with who actually lives here, composing the one group not disposed to spontaneous self-deception, Sandinista manipulation, utopia-seeking, or just plain hatred of America. On the flight back to Miami, my seatmate, a middle-aged Nicaraguan woman off to visit her children who have gone to Miami to live, asked me, "When are you Americans going to help us?" Then, lapsing into Spanish, she said, "Rambo es bueno."

David Brock is a writer for Insight, *a weekly newsmagazine.*

"The Central Americans' peace process is on a roll."

The Arias Plan Can Bring Peace to Central America

Karl Bermann

When the presidents of the five Central American republics began their summit meeting in Guatemala City Aug. 6, [1987], there seemed little reason for hope that they would actually sign Costa Rican President Oscar Arias' regional peace plan. Just days before, with great fanfare, Ronald Reagan had unveiled his own "peace plan" for Central America, and that announcement, it was said, had thrown the Central Americans' parley into chaos.

Their summit had already been postponed once as a result of behind-the-scenes arm-twisting by the Reagan administration, which clearly opposed the Arias plan. In addition, the Central American peace effort had four years of disappointed hopes behind it: Its predecessor, the Contadora initiative sponsored by Mexico, Venezuela, Colombia and Panama, had repeatedly met with failure as El Salvador and Honduras bowed to pressure from their U.S. patron and withdrew support at the crucial moment.

But this time, much to everyone's surprise, the Central Americans did sign a peace pact, and for the moment, at least, it seems to be working like a contagion, confounding the skeptics and overcoming one seemingly insurmountable obstacle after another.

The Sandinistas have allowed *La Prensa* and Radio Católica to reopen and have appointed one of their sternest critics, Cardinal Miguel Obando y Bravo, to head a National Reconciliation Commission. In El Salvador, President Jose Napoleon Duarte and the FMLN [Farabundo Marti National Liberation Front] guerrillas have reopened the negotiations they broke off nearly three years ago. The government of Guatemala is talking to that country's rebels for the first time, with the two sides already announcing a cease-fire. And Honduras, which gave the world the

Karl Bermann, "Whether to be pro peace or contra peace plan in Central America," *National Catholic Reporter,* October 30, 1987. Copyright 1987, Karl Bermann. Reprinted with the author's permission.

term "banana republic," is pledging to buck the Reagan administration and kick out the contras.

For those who have followed Central America's escalating conflicts and militarization these past several years, such signs would be hopeful enough. But there is another, perhaps more important, dynamic unleashed by the Guatemala accord. The hopes and expectations that its initial successes have engendered are adding fuel to the peace process—despite the deep differences that divide them, few Central Americans have been able to avoid getting caught up in it. The momentum is such that no faction or party, whatever its misgivings, wants or can afford to be seen as the cause of the agreement's failure. . . .

Juncture of Historic Trends

The achievement of a peace accord by the Central Americans themselves marks the juncture of two historic trends. On the one hand, there is the movement among Latins in recent years toward greater independence and assertiveness in world affairs. This tendency can be seen in the growing Latin solidarity on the debt question and in the launching of the Contadora initiative itself. On the other hand is the long-term decline of U.S. influence in Latin America, a process that has accelerated greatly during the era of Reaganism.

The paternalism that for so long characterized Uncle Sam's relationship with Latin America, symbolized by the "big stick" and the Monroe Doctrine, simply doesn't work any longer. Whatever authority the Reagan administration's Central America policy did command internationally has vanished in the wake of the Iran-contra affair. Outside the United States, the scandal has popped the Reagan bubble and thrown into serious question the future of its policy. The administration is now isolated as never before, supported in its approach to Central America, as Costa Rican President Arias reportedly told Reagan during a recent meeting, only by Grenda.

While the White House may be as willing as ever to defend the Reagan Doctrine to the last drop of Central American blood, the natives are deserting. Even the most slavishly dependent of Central American leaders, such as El Salvador's Duarte, feel both the need and the freedom to cast loose from U.S. policy and make their own way. Central Americans have simply come to the conclusion that, despite the enormous differences that divide them, they all have too much to lose to continue on a course of escalating military conflict and confrontation.

"Unlike the Central Americans, those staffing the administration in Washington are immune to the peace euphoria."

The peace plan designed by Arias contains touches of genius—the very points that have drawn the most fire from critics. While the right says it provides no guarantee that Nicaragua will "democratize" or distance itself from the Soviet bloc, and elements of the left criticize it for applying the same cease-fire/negotiation formula to the differing situations of insurgency extant in Nicaragua, El Salvador and Guatemala, these "neutral" provisions are what made agreement possible.

They are not really neutral, however, only algebraic. They allow for, and ultimately require, each country to assign specific values to the plan's variables based on its own particular situation. Thus, although the accord requires no government to sit down with insurgents, the realities of El Salvador dictate that Duate must negotiate with the FMLN-FDR [Democratic Revolutionary Front], while the Nicaraguan government may well be able to ignore the contra leaders, who have little following outside Washington and Miami.

This is not the first time Central Americans have demonstrated that they can be adroit diplomatists. Perhaps that is because—to borrow a metaphor from former Guatemalan President Juan José Arévalo—in a sea of sharks, it is the sardines who must live by their wits. In 1907, in circumstances of strife very similar to the present, Central American foreign ministers met in Washington at the invitation of Theodore Roosevelt and Mexican President Porfirio Díaz. Then, too, they negotiated a comprehensive agreement for non-interference in each other's affairs, including the establishment of an arbitration court to settle their disputes. The 1907 accord succeeded in bringing peace to the region—that is,

until the incoming Taft administration in the United States sabotaged it two years later by underwriting an insurgency to oust a nationalist government in Nicaragua.

US Caught off Guard

As remarkable as it may seem, U.S. officials have now been charging that their erstwhile Central American allies signed the Guatemala plan out of concern for their own "narrow, nationalistic interests." Given their previous claims to be defending those same Central American interests, that they can even think of such a charge illustrates the extent to which the Reagan administration's policy has set it adrift from the real world.

Unlike the Central Americans, those staffing the administration in Washington are immune to the peace euphoria, perhaps because they are comfortably removed from the effects of the war and can, from the vantage point of the country club, better appreciate the ideological fine points of a crusade against communism.

In any event, the signing of the peace plan caught the Reaganites off guard. In the past they pulled strings with their allies to thwart any agreement that would leave the Sandinista experiment in Nicaragua essentially intact. And that is what the current plan does. It recognizes "the right to all nations to freely determine, without outside interference of any kind, their economic, political and social model."

While this provision may sound reasonable enough, the Reagan administration has not altered one iota its determination to overthrow the Sandinistas. And to add insult to injury for the traditional Yankee supremacists at the State Department, the Central Americans' agreement leaves the monitoring of compliance entirely in the hands of Latin Americans.

Political considerations have made the administration reluctant to openly oppose the Guatemala plan. It has always had to sweeten its requests for contra funding by claiming that it pursues a "two-track" policy, combining military pressure with the search for a negotiated solution. But Reagan and his spokespersons have become more critical of the peace agreement with each new sign of progress in Central America.

The State Department has, for example, denounced Nicaragua's reopening of *La Prensa* and Radio Católica as mere "cosmetic reforms," notwithstanding that it previously pointed to their closure as prime evidence of the Sandinistas' incorrigible "totalitarianism."

Squeezing Central Americans

Behind the scenes, meanwhile, U.S. diplomats have been working feverishly to find a means to scuttle the agreement. Costa Rican officials say the Reagan administration has tried to exert pressure on Arias to alter his interpretation of what steps the peace plan requires Nicaragua to take. Other Central American leaders have felt the squeeze as well. Even Cardinal Obando told reporters that he has come under intense pressure to quit his post as head of Nicaragua's Reconciliation Commission, although he declined to identify its source. . . .

Administration spokespersons, in interviews with the *New York Times*, recently elaborated a series of conditions they said the Sandinistas have to meet before they will withdraw the contra aid request. The list included demands that Nicaragua change its constitutionally mandated election timetable, immediately end all military assistance from the Soviet bloc or Cuba, disband the neighborhood Sandinista defense committees and, in Reagan's own words, ''allow . . . a free economy.''

Such requirements go way beyond the Guatemala plan and are completely inconsistent with it. They were clearly put forward in the expectation that they would be rejected. But as with each succeeding ploy the administration has used in its effort to torpedo the peace agreement, this one backfired, forcing, it appears, yet another change of tactics. House Speaker Jim Wright, who had been observing his own cease-fire with the White House, immediately denounced the new conditions as ''ridiculous demands that violate Nicaraguan sovereignty.''

The attempt by Congress and the administration to avoid confrontation over Central America . . . conceals what is likely the deepest foreign policy rift in governing circles since Vietnam. In fact, with the Central American peace initiative coming in the aftermath of Contragate, the Reaganites' tough talk may not be just hot air—their Central America policy may be irrelevant. . . .

Peace Process on a Roll

There is still a long way to go before the hopes raised by the peace plan become reality, and it is a route more heavily mined than the Persian Gulf. There are deep political and social divisions that no agreement, no matter how well-crafted, can paper over. And even if the current mood of pacific euphoria succeeds in bringing Central America's discordant political factions into harmony, the antagonisms spawned by the region's miasmic social inequalities will remain.

''The main threat to Central American peace still resides in Washington.''

But for the short term, the main threat to Central American peace still resides in Washington. There, the ghost of Joseph McCarthy still stalks, and who can say for certain that the congresspeople now riding on President Arias' coattails will not yet succumb to the fear of being charged with ''losing'' Central America? The halls of Congress, after all, may not in the end prove fertile ground for the spirit of independence that is making such headway south of the border. U.S. legislators can yet kill the prospects for peace by resuscitating the contras.

But, for the moment, the Central Americans' peace process is on a roll. It can't solve every problem, but it can allow the region to find its own equilibrium. And it's just possible that the ties of goodwill it is spreading everywhere will bind its enemies harmless like the Lilliputians' thousand threads bound Gulliver.

Karl Bermann is a historian and the author of Under the Big Stick: Nicaragua and the United States Since 1848.

"A time frame for compliance [with the Arias plan] was provided. Now time has run out."

The Arias Plan Cannot Bring Peace to Central America

Jeane Kirkpatrick

Editor's note: The following viewpoint is in two parts. Both Part I and Part II are by Jeane Kirkpatrick.

I

Will the government of Nicaragua comply with the terms of the agreement it signed at Esquipulas [the Arias plan]? Will the government stand aside while Radio Catolica broadcasts news as well as prayers and the dozen other radio stations shut down by the FSLN [Sandinista National Liberation Front] comandantes go back on the air? Will the opposition parties be able to hold meetings and peaceful marches without disruption? Will the government negotiate a cease fire with the resistance (the contras)? Will it free nine to ten thousand political prisoners held in Nicaragua's jails? . . .

That, finally, is the issue in Nicaragua and elsewhere in Central America: whether governments and groups contending for power (including Marxist-Leninists and "death squads") are willing to work out the future of their country without killing, kidnapping and taking hostage those with different ideas about what that future should be. The Central American accords commit the governments of the region to amnesty, free expression, assembly and elections—to internal dialogue and external peace. The accords, however, do not commit them to any particular economic, social or political form of organization but to a particular political method—to the method of dialogue and consent rather than the method of violence. And in politics, as George Orwell wrote, the choice of method is the definitive act.

The Sandinistas are not finding it easy to forgo force in dealing with opponents. Eight days after the accords were signed, police with dogs, batons and electric cattle prods broke up a peaceful

Jeane Kirkpatrick, "Is Nicaragua Ready to Comply with Pact?" *Conservative Chronicle*, November 4, 1987.
Jeane Kirkpatrick, "Nicaraguan Contradictions Cloud Peace Plan," *Conservative Chronicle*, January 3, 1988. Reprinted with the author's permission.

demonstration and arrested and jailed the president of Nicaragua's bar association and the head of the Nicaraguan human rights commission. The clear purpose was to intimidate not only those who participated in the march but all those who were aware of what happened to the marchers.

A week later, 18 Nicaraguan youths were arrested en route to an anniversary celebration of the Social Christian Party in Managua. They were tried and some are still in jail. Again the clear purpose was intimidation.

Outside Managua arbitrary arrests of campesinos continue unabated.

The habits of violence and intimidation are strong in Nicaragua. They are sustained by the Sandinista comandantes' belief that force is an acceptable method for dealing with fellow Nicaraguans. Obviously they find it morally permissible to govern by force—they are part of a great world revolution which itself proceeds mainly by force.

Humanizing Opponents

When Daniel Ortega spoke at the U.N. General Assembly [in 1987], he commenced by noting that it was the 20th anniversary of the death of Che Guevara. Ortega said that like Gandhi and Christ, Che "left everything to work for the people." Ortega seems not to have noticed that unlike Gandhi and Christ, Che Guevara chose violence as his method of "working" for the people. The reminder came from Bolivia and El Salvador where other guerrillas commemorated Che's anniversary with bombings. Ortega seems not to understand that while Christ and Gandhi affirmed the humanity of all, the method of violence requires dehumanizing opponents—seeing them as traitors, mercenaries, counterrevolutionaries, collaborationists, not as fellow citizens with different ideas about how best to live together.

Herein lies the reason that the dialogue prescribed

by the accords is so crucial. The very act of discussing an issue with an opponent humanizes him. It gives respect both to the individual and his opinions. This is the reason, doubtless, that the government of Nicaragua has so far refused discussion with the leaders of the Nicaraguan resistance.

It is also the reason that El Salvador's president, Napoleon Duarte, acted immediately to initiate negotiations with El Salvador's guerrilla forces, the FMLN [Farabundo Marti National Liberation Front]. Duarte refuses to dehumanize, refuses to hate even the man whom he knows planned and supervised the kidnapping of his daughter. Duarte is therefore always ready to make peace with El Salvador's guerrillas.

"There are no institutional processes available to open Nicaragua's political system."

In El Salvador, it is the guerrillas who are reluctant to talk peace.

"Our confidence is in the total struggle of our people," said FMLN chief and communist party leader Shafik Handal. "When the struggle has developed further there will be new possibilities for a just solution." For Marxists in El Salvador as in Nicaragua "struggle"—that is violence—is the preferred, "historically correct" method.

But in signing the Central American accords Daniel Ortega committed himself not only to democratic ends but to democratic means. He committed himself to eschewing violent "struggle" against the people of Nicaragua.

Now he is stuck with that commitment.

II

The Central American peace accord signed in Guatemala [the Arias plan] was a plan, not just an expression of good intentions. It committed its signatories, the five presidents of Central America, to establish authentic democratic processes and carry out national reconciliation. A time frame for compliance was provided. Now time has run out.

When the presidents met in Costa Rica to examine the question of compliance, it was clear to all (except possibly Daniel Ortega) that Nicaragua had not fulfilled its promises. There had been no general amnesty, no cease fire, no internal reconciliation. Controls over speech, press and assembly had been relaxed, but freedom in all domains remained sharply limited. Central America's presidents said as much. Now they said Nicaragua must either comply or give up the pretense. . . .

An interesting and often contradictory scramble

has ensued in Nicaragua, making it clear that the Sandinistas do not relish the choice with which they are confronted.

Sandinistas Not Consistent

"Nicaragua cancels State of Emergency," the *Washington Post* announced on Page 1. "Five More in Nicaraguan Opposition Are Arrested by the Security Police," the *New York Times* said on the same page on the same day. Both headlines were accurate.

On the same day that Managua announced the lifting of a state of emergency, police arrested leaders of Nicaragua's democratic trade unions, private sector, independent press and democratic political parties. They were interrogated for some 36 hours and released.

This was not the first time opposition leaders were arrested at the same time the goverment sought to convince the world of its democratization. It also happened eight days after the signing of the accords, when the Nicaraguan government forcibly broke up a peaceful demonstration and arrested Lino Hernandez, director of the independent Permanent Commission on Human Rights, and Alberto Saborio, president of the Nicaraguan Bar Association. Both arrests were clearly designed to intimidate.

Now Hernandez, Saborio and 10 associates once again are victims of the Sandinista desire to proclaim freedom and control its use.

Sandinistas' Style of Democracy

It is not the only contradiction. An amnesty was declared for 3,500 political prisoners *providing* they are accepted by the United States. While the state of emergency was lifted and the constitution restored, official newspaper *Barricada* warned the restoration of civil rights "should not be misinterpreted as a blank check for irresponsibility and subversion."

"They are telling us that this is their style of democracy," said *La Prensa* Director Violetta Chamorro, whose brother-in-law, *La Prensa* Editor Jaime Chamorro, was arrested.

Is this "style of democracy" acceptable to the U.S. congressmen who have tied their support for aid to the contras to Nicaragua's compliance with the Central American accords? . . . Democratic leaders have indicated they will make an all-out effort to block further aid to the contras. They call their policy "a risk for peace."

But it is necessary to ask what is being risked.

Is there a chance for democracy in Nicaragua without continued pressure on these would-be totalitarians?

Is there a chance for peace in El Salvador while the Sandinista regime rules Nicaragua?

Is there a chance for economic development in Central America while the region is thus afflicted for repression, revolution and civil war?

Is there any good reason for Democrats who do

not desire a Communist Central America to oppose aid to the contras?

But opponents of aid have a question of their own: Is it morally justifiable for those who believe in peace and democracy to support the use of force by Nicaraguans against the Nicaraguan government?

Need To Support Contras

El Salvador's president, Napoleon Duarte, provided the answer to this last question in a speech before the United Nations General Assembly:

"Force can only be acceptable," Duarte argued, "when there are no institutional processes available to open the political system, and then should only be used for the purpose of opening that system."

Supporters of democracy must agree. There are no institutional processes available to open Nicaragua's political system. It is therefore up to Congress to help the rulers of Nicaragua understand that democracy is their only alternative.

Jeane Kirkpatrick is a syndicated columnist and a former US ambassador to the United Nations.

"The conflict between Israeli and Palestinian is being shaped by . . . competing, centuries-old claims to the same precious strip of land."

Israelis and Palestinians: A Historical Overview

Marc D. Charney

In the West Bank, Gaza and Jerusalem, the conflict between Israeli and Palestinian is being shaped by a fratricidal agony: competing, centuries-old claims to the same precious strip of land between the Jordan River and the Mediterranean, and the right to exist there as a nation.

The rivalry is as old as the contest between Moslem and Jew for the legacy of their common father, Abraham. Which people should own the land where the Temple stood, or Mohammed ascended to heaven—or, for that matter, where Abraham himself is buried?

But the rivalry is also distinctly modern. For the precise lines on the modern map of the Middle East—the lines that divide the West Bank and Gaza from Israel, and define Israel itself—were drawn only in the 20th century. They reflect the breakup of the Ottoman Empire and the rise of Arab nationalism, an inward rush of Jews to flee pogroms and the Holocaust, the displacement of hundreds of thousands of Arabs, and the seemingly intractable conflict that continues. In part, the map was drawn to suit the interests of powers outside the region; but it was also forged in round after round of local warfare—a resort to arms when ambiguous promises and agreements failed to tame hatred and suspicion.

The Question of Land

Jews who assert that Israel should keep control of all the land between the Jordan and the Mediterranean often cite God's promise to Abraham, invoking a vision of a land they controlled intermittently before the destruction of the Second Temple in A.D. 70; Israelis also cite a modern claim to secure borders, saying it could mean suicide to give up this land without first obtaining peace and a formal recognition by its neighbors of Israel's right

to exist as a Jewish state.

For the Arabs, this is a land their people have lived on for centuries, and for the thousands of refugees the Israeli occupation of the West Bank— the ancient Jewish lands of Judea and Samaria—and Gaza is now made more bitter by tribal memory, passed on from generation to generation.

If for centuries Jews longed to return to Jerusalem, today thousands of Palestinians cherish a vision of rocky villages and citrus groves that they left when conflict broke out with the Jews in 1948. What the Jews call Eretz Israel, they call Palestine. For many of these, it is not a question of a West Bank state for Palestinians, but the dissolution of the Israeli state—a point in the Palestine Liberation Organization charter that the P.L.O. has never renounced. The current protests have brought forward some Palestinians willing to say they would recognize Israel's right to exist if that would bring an independent state. But they have been unwilling to renounce the leadership of the P.L.O., with which Israel will not negotiate; if anything, the attitude of the current young leaders of the protest appears even more radical.

The precise boundaries of the disputed land today are, for the most part, limits defined by Britain under a mandate approved by the League of Nations in 1922 after Britain and France divided up power over the Middle East territories that the Ottoman Empire held before World War I. Under the Ottomans, Palestine had been administered as a section of Syria, and it was in this period that Zionist Jews began immigrating in the late 19th century, in large part in response to pogroms in Russia. Nevertheless, by the end of World War I Arabs still constituted more than 90 percent of the population.

When Britain was granted the mandate, a central condition was that it foster the creation of a Jewish national homeland in Palestine, as long as this did not prejudice the rights of those already living in the

Marc D. Charney, "The Battleground from the Jordan to the Sea," *The New York Times*, February 28, 1988. Copyright © 1988 by The New York Times Company. Reprinted by permission.

area. The promise was in the Balfour Declaration, a letter written in November 1917, in which Britain, seeking Jewish help in its war effort, had promised Lord Rothschild, president of the British Zionist Federation, that it would work for a Jewish homeland in Palestine.

Undefined Boundaries

The mandate and the Balfour Declaration became central pillars for the Jewish claim to the land that is now Israel. These documents did not, however, spell out boundaries for a Jewish homeland within Palestine or define the form it should take. Britain, meanwhile, had made another promise during World War I, in a letter sent in 1915 by Sir Henry McMahon, Britain's high commissioner in Egypt, to Hussein, Hashemite Sherif of Mecca, in hopes of encouraging the Arab revolt that later broke out against the Ottomans. This letter pledged British support for Arab independence in the area, but left ambiguous whether this included Palestine.

"Many Arabs say they were driven off their land by war . . . and have a right to return to all of it. The Israelis say that this claim means the Arabs are arguing . . . for the destruction of Israel itself."

Over the next 20 years, Jewish immigration and acquisition of land became the central issues in a growing conflict between Arabs and Jews—particularly in the 1930's, when Britain tried to stem the flow. In 1936, Arabs staged a general strike that was followed by an uprising that lasted until 1939. It included bitter Arab attacks on Jews in Hebron, Haifa, Jaffa and Tel Aviv, and prompted a strengthening of Jewish self-defense groups. In May 1939, with war imminent, the British published a White Paper that effectively promised the Arabs a halt to the flow of Jews after five years, to be followed by self-government with an Arab majority. The Zionists were outraged. By 1947, despite continuing British efforts to restrict immigration, a Jewish population that had been 56,000 in the early 1920's had grown to 650,000—two-fifths of the population of Palestine—and the United Nations split the land into Jewish and Arab countries.

Partition and War

The map, as drawn by the United Nations, divided the land into six sectors—three Arab, three Jewish, with Jerusalem reserved as an international zone well within the largest Arab sector. The Jewish leadership in Palestine accepted partition; the Arab leadership did not.

In the fighting that developed as the date of partition approached, and in the invasion by neighboring Arab countries that followed, the Jews made major gains, including the modern city of Jerusalem, although the Old City and the Wailing Wall fell under Jordanian control. The fighting also established a pattern of Arab displacement and bitterness that lasted 40 years, erupting again [in] December [1987] in sustained violence in the occupied territories. Today, many Arabs say they were driven off their land by war and by aggressive land acquisition policies, and have a right to return to all of it. The Israelis say that this claim means the Arabs are arguing not for the West Bank and Gaza or even the existence of a Palestinian state, but for the destruction of Israel itself.

Israelis maintain that Arab moderates who might agree to recognize Israel's right to exist in return for a homeland carved out of the occupied lands have been intimidated by the popularity of the militant positions of the P.L.O. The Israelis would prefer a state federated with Jordan, not an independent one. Moderate Palestinians say Israeli occupation policies have prevented the emergence of popular moderate leaders. The immediate causes for the refugee flight of 1948 before the advancing forces are disputed, and most historical accounts cite a combination of factors.

The cease-fire lines of 1949 set the frontiers of Israel as it was to exist until 1967. Jordan, whose Arab Legion had fought in the 1948 war, held until the 1967 war the area now known as the West Bank, as well as East Jerusalem, including the holy sites in the Old City, from which Jews were barred. The Gaza Strip fell under Egyptian administration. But during all those years neither Egypt nor Jordan fostered the creation of a Palestinian nation in these territories. The West Bank, in fact, became incorporated into Jordan.

Angry Lesson at Suez

The refugee centers in Syria, Jordan and the Gaza Strip became sources for Palestinian raids on Israel, prompting retaliatory raids by Israel. In 1956, Israel cooperated with Britain and France in overrunning Gaza and Sinai while the British and French occupied the Suez Canal. But international pressure—notably from the United States—forced a pullback without a peace agreement with Egypt. Israelis drew an angry lesson from this. After the fighting in 1967, they were determined that future withdrawals must bring peace.

This time their armies seized, in addition to Sinai, the Golan Heights, all of the West Bank, and the Arab part of Jerusalem, including the Old City. East Jerusalem was annexed almost immediately, the city was declared Israel's capital and the Golan Heights was annexed in 1981. Some one million Arabs who remained in the West Bank and Gaza Strip were compelled to live under Israeli military administration.

In November 1967, the United Nations had passed Resolution 242, envisioning, as a basis for future peace negotiations, a withdrawal by Israel from occupied Arab lands in exchange for peace and recognition of Israel's right to exist. The resolution left a central ambiguity, however, in failing to specify how much territory would be evacuated. It also referred only to refugees, rather than to a Palestinian nation—a point at the core of the P.L.O.'s refusal to accept Resolution 242 as a sole basis for negotiations.

"Israel refuses to negotiate with the P.L.O., . . . preferring instead to deal with other Palestinians. . . . But these Palestinians are reluctant to take the step of entering any negotiations without the participation or approval of the P.L.O."

Israel has since withdrawn completely from Egyptian land in Sinai under terms of the Camp David treaty signed with Egypt in 1979. But reaching a solution over the Gaza Strip and West Bank has proven vastly more difficult. Sites in the West Bank in particular are linked to the Jewish past. And the land, with its strategic hills, long border and proximity to the coastal cities, is critical to Israeli military planning. In any comprehensive negotiations, the question of Jerusalem would be the most difficult of all, because of its religious significance for Moslems as well as for Jews, and because Israel insists its annexation is irrevocable.

Ambiguities

At the same time as the Camp David peace treaty was drawn up, Egypt and Israel reached accord on a framework for a Palestinian settlement: a five-year transition period intended to lead to "autonomy" for Palestinians in the West Bank and Gaza. But again, a central ambiguity was left, this time on the question of what autonomy meant. The Arabs interpreted it to mean statehood, the Israelis limited self-rule.

The question of who should negotiate for the Palestinians is crucial; until it is answered, no settlement is likely. Israel refuses to negotiate with the P.L.O., on the ground that it is a terrorist organization, preferring instead to deal with other Palestinians and with King Hussein of Jordan. But these Palestinians are reluctant to take the step of entering any negotiations without the participation or approval of the P.L.O.

Meanwhile, Israel has been busy establishing its own presence in the territories it occupied, changing their character by establishing military camps and Jewish settlements. At first, Labor Governments attempted to limit the pattern of settlement to one that more heavily reflected security concerns than links to history, appearing to leave room for territorial compromise. After 1977, when the right-wing Likud bloc came to power, encouragement was given to groups that seek to retain all the occupied territories as part of the ancient land of Israel.

By late [1987], it seemed that the Arab world had begun to pay less attention to the Palestinians. But in December [1987], a new phase of the fratricidal agony opened—the rocks and firebombs of a frustrated new Palestinian generation. Defense Minister Yitzhak Rabin, who has become the spokesman for Israeli determination to put down the unrest, declared: "We have to drive home to their minds and hearts: 'By violence you'll gain nothing.'" But youthful protesters in Gaza seemed to express how difficult that might be. "Kill us all," they taunted Israeli soldiers as they stoned them. "Come and kill us all or get out."

Marc D. Charney is a staff writer with The New York Times.

Israel Should Withdraw from the West Bank

Michael Lerner

The widespread moral outrage at Israel's policies in Gaza and the West Bank—the sense that Israel is violating the basic ethical values of Judaism—is coupled with a growing realization that these policies are also bad for Israel and bad for the Jewish people. Granted, some of Israel's critics have been unfair, both in their failure to acknowledge the role of Palestinian leaders and Arab states in creating the conflict, and in their tendency to judge Israel by standards that they rarely apply to the rest of the world. Nevertheless, from the standpoint of Jewish ethics and Jewish survival the occupation is unacceptable. There are plausible solutions to the Palestinian problem that must be tried. But they won't be tried unless American Jews unequivocally tell Israel that the occupation cannot continue. This message must be conveyed forcefully to Prime Minister Shamir and to the Israeli public.

The pain and sorrow many American Jews feel about Israel's policies on the West Bank and Gaza are rooted deep in our collective memory as a people. Israel's attempt to regain control of the refugee camps by denying food to hundreds of thousands of men, women, and children, by raiding homes and dragging out their occupants in the middle of the night to stand for hours in the cold, by savagely beating a civilian population and breaking its bones—these activities are deplorable to any civilized human being. That they are done by a Jewish state is both tragic and inexcusable. We did not survive the gas chambers and crematoria so that we could become the oppressors of Gaza. The Israeli politicians who have led us into this morass are desecrating the legacy of Jewish history. If Jewish tradition has stood for anything, it has stood for the principle that justice must triumph over violence.

For that reason, we typically have sided with the oppressed and have questioned the indiscriminate use of force. We, who love Israel, who remain proud Zionists, are outraged at the betrayal of this sacred legacy by small-minded Israeli politicians who feel more comfortable with the politics of repression than with the search for peace.

Rejecting Israel's Tactics

Any policy that requires the immoral tactics being used against an unarmed and militarily subjugated population must be rejected. If the activities of the Israeli army really are necessary, that in itself would be sufficient to discredit the occupation. We do not diminish our loyalty to our own people by acknowledging our profound sadness at the suffering of Palestinians. Those who have grown up in camps or in exile have experienced homelessness in much the same way that Jews have experienced it throughout history. Even if this suffering were the absolutely necessary consequence of our self-preservation, we would still be deeply upset by the pain that thereby was caused to another group of human beings. We have been too sensitized by our own history of oppression not to feel diminished when others are in pain. That is why we dip drops from our wine cups at the Passover seder in memory of the pain of our Egyptian slaveholders. But when that pain is largely unnecessary, we feel not only sadness but also anger and a deep determination to do what we can to stop the suffering.

Our outrage is shared by many Israelis. Over fifty thousand of them gathered in Tel Aviv on January 23 [1988] in one of the biggest antiwar demonstrations in Jewish history to protest Israel's policies. Joined by hundreds of thousands of others who could not attend the demonstration but who share their outrage, they are asking American Jews to speak out. To be silent, or keep our criticisms safely "in the family," would be to betray our Israeli brothers and

Michael Lerner, "The Occupation: Immoral and Stupid," *Tikkun*, March/April 1988. Reprinted with permission.

sisters.

That is why we say in unequivocal terms to the Israeli government: Stop the beatings, stop the breaking of bones, stop the late night raids on people's homes, stop the use of food as a weapon of war, stop pretending that you can respond to an entire people's agony with guns and blows and power. Publicly acknowledge that the Palestinians have the same right to national self-determination that we Jews have, and negotiate a solution with representatives of the Palestinians!

But our anger at Israel's policies comes not only from moral outrage but also from deep concern about Israel's survival and the survival of the Jewish people. From a strictly self-interested position, the occupation is stupid. Here's why:

1) The longer the occupation exists, the more angry and radical young Palestinians will become. The possibility of negotiating a two-state solution will decrease since these young Palestinians will come to regard a West Bank state as a "sell-out" of their dreams for a fully liberated Palestine, and PLO [Palestine Liberation Organization] leaders willing to settle for a such a state will be seen not as "moderates" but as betrayers of the struggle. This attitude is becoming more prevalent, but it has not yet achieved dominance. Yitzhak Rabin's policy of "the iron fist" only quickens this radicalization. In years to come we may wish that we had dealt with the PLO before the Palestinians embraced some radical form of Islamic fundamentalism that makes it a religious sin to live in peace with Israel.

2) Even those Palestinians who live within the pre-1967 borders of Israel are being drawn into the struggle. Faced with the repression of their own people in the occupied territories, they participated in the general strike in December [1987]. Some have rioted in protest of Israeli military action. The longer the occupation lasts, the more they will be drawn into the struggle—with disastrous consequences for Israel. Unless the occupation is speedily ended, Israel may soon resemble Beirut or Northern Ireland.

A Dangerous Shift to the Right

3) As the occupation continues, the logic of domination and repression of Palestinians will require that Israelis adopt an increasingly insensitive view towards those whom they must control. Israelis will inevitably be pushed to the political right. In the past few years we have seen the right-wing Tehiyah party and even some sectors of Likud advocate Kahane-like ideas. Today, right-wing members of the Labor party such as Yitzhak Rabin act in ways that would have made them scream at Ariel Sharon only a few years ago. This move to the right is likely to accelerate the already large emigration ("yeridah") rate plaguing Israel—only this time those who leave will be going, not to find their "fortune" in America,

but to escape a political situation that they cannot morally justify. Increasingly, it will be the scientific, technical, and professional personnel who leave—people whose contributions have been essential to the defense technology, economic strength, and intellectual creativity of the country.

"The occupation threatens to erode the popular base of support for Israel in the United States."

---

4) Because most of the pro-Zionist Jewish leadership in the United States has remained quiet, the only voices articulating clear moral criticism have been those of Israel's enemies. For the anti-Semites and the anti-Zionists these are wonderful times. Reports already exist of campus demonstrations with posters denouncing "Jewish murderers"—and many Jewish college students, ashamed of the images of the Jewish state being portrayed in the media every day, are willing, for the first time, to listen to the anti-Zionist propaganda being disseminated. Previously lacking any rational foundation for their attacks on Jews, the voices of hate have gained credibility by their association with legitimate criticisms of the Jewish state. Israel's policies give credibility to the worst lies about Judaism. And, in the years ahead, the Jewish people may face hard times based not simply on lies and distortions of anti-Semites, but on the justified indignation of many people who see the Jewish state embodying a viciousness and moral callousness that they would find repugnant anywhere.

Eroding Moral Image

5) The occupation threatens to erode the popular base of support for Israel in the United States. As America's economic problems intensify in the coming years, people will inevitably question any large-scale military and economic aid given to any foreign country. Moreover, major American corporations have never been happy with the government's tilt toward Israel. Most corporations understand that their long-term economic interests are better served by friendlier relations with the various Arab autocracies. Opportunities for investment and trade have been limited by America's alliance with Israel. The United States's policy of military support to Israel is one instance in which popular forces, using the democratic mechanisms of the electoral process, have countered corporate interests. Even the power of AIPAC [American Israel Public Affairs Committee] is based less on its fund-raising capacities (does anyone seriously doubt that Arab oil companies could, if they so chose, raise more cash for political

candidates than AIPAC?) than on its ability to mobilize a political constituency of Israel's supporters. Yet many of Israel's supporters would be much less committed if Israel were perceived as having repudiated its commitment to democratic values and human rights. If Americans continue to be barraged by images of Israelis beating, tear-gassing, shooting, and starving a civilian population, they will be much less likely to stand up to the Arab and corporate interests that argue for "evenhandedness" in American policy.

Make no mistake about it—what is at stake for Israel is not only its Jewish soul but its survival. Once the perception fades that Israel stands for moral values, those of us who want to provide for Israel's defense may be unable to convince the United States to supply the latest and most sophisticated military hardware, and Israel may be unable to keep up with Arab armies supplied not only by the Soviet Union but also by Japan and Europe. As a result, Israel may be vulnerable to serious military attack. There is no more pressing Israeli security need than its need to maintain its image as a society committed to just values.

6) The occupation is also a threat to the survival of Judaism and the Jewish people in the Diaspora. The breakdown of authoritarian communal structures increasingly makes every Jew a Jew by choice. In the past two decades there has been a dramatic revival of interest in Judaism from Americans who have found the individualistic and competitive values of American society unfulfilling and morally vacuous. They have turned to Judaism because they rightly sense Judaism's moral sensitivity and its transcendent vision, which stands in sharp opposition to the logic of domination and mean-spiritedness that permeates life in most competitive market societies. The occupation may reverse this trend since increasing numbers of Jews will begin to dismiss much of Judaism's moral vision as pious moralizing that lacks substance. A Judaism that has lost its moral teeth and becomes an apologist for every Israeli policy, no matter what its moral content, is a Judaism that not only betrays the prophetic tradition, but also risks losing the adherence of the Jewish people. . . .

Solutions Are Possible

There are solutions to these problems. A demilitarized and politically neutral Palestinian state can be established on the West Bank and Gaza in precisely the same fashion that the Russians and Americans agreed to give Austria independence after WWII. Demilitarization would be guaranteed by the United States and the Soviet Union, and the treaty that establishes this Palestinian state would also recognize Israel's right to intervene militarily in order to prevent the introduction of tanks, heavy artillery, or airplanes. The United States, Soviet

Union, and Israel would create a unified force to protect the Palestinian state from attack by Syria, Iraq, Iran, or other hostile powers, and the United States would enter into a collective security agreement with Israel guaranteeing the full power of American military might to defend Israel against attack. The Palestinian state would renounce all claims to the rest of Palestine and would police those remaining Palestinians still desiring a further struggle with Israel. Israel would agree to enter into economic confederation with this Palestinian state after a specified period of peaceful coexistence.

Who could negotiate for the Palestinians? Any group that is willing to recognize Israel's right to exist. If Israel claims that the PLO doesn't represent the Palestinians in the occupied territories, let it immediately hold a plebiscite to determine whom West Bank Palestinians want to negotiate for them. And Israel must set no restrictions on who can be a candidate.

"There are solutions to these problems. A demilitarized and politically neutral Palestinian state can be established on the West Bank and Gaza."

What if no Palestinian leadership is willing to accept a demilitarized Palestinian state? Then Israel loses nothing by having offered, and actually gains a great deal. Instead of Israeli rejectionism, we would be back to a clear picture of the Palestinians as the obstacle. It is reasonable for Israel to insist on its own security. If, in the 1930s, Jews had been offered a state under a similar plan guaranteed by all the great powers, they certainly would have accepted it, even on a considerably smaller piece of land. Ultimately, a totally demilitarized Middle East is optimum, but for now a demilitarized Palestinian state is the only kind of state likely to be accepted. We hope the Palestinians prove the skeptics wrong by accepting a demilitarized state.

Make Them an Offer

Israel should publicly offer the Palestinians such a state now. This proclamation will help ensure Israel's political and military survival. It probably also will provoke a crisis in the Palestinian world and bring to the fore the unresolved conflict between those Palestinians who really are willing to accept Israel's right to exist and those who desire a state on the West Bank simply as a launching pad for the total destruction of Israel. If the rejectionists win the struggle, Israel has proved itself reasonable without weakening itself militarily. We hope, however, that the forces of reason among the Palestinians will win and that the kind of peace that most Israelis want can be achieved.

Anything less than such a public proclamation will be seen as stalling—and rightly so. Prime Minister Shamir's attempts to revive Camp David "autonomy" talks clearly are delay tactics. The autonomy being proposed is a sham—the opposite of genuine self-determination. But even an international conference will have limited impact if Israel is unwilling to commit itself to a demilitarized Palestinian state. A "solution" that proposes anything less than this—for example, a Jordanian confederation on the West Bank under which the Palestinians still do not have self-determination, their own flag, or their own passports—will give extremist Palestinians the incentive to expand the struggle. The psychology of the situation is clear: Until the Palestinians feel that they own something, which limited autonomy cannot provide, they have no real incentive to stop the struggle. Once they achieve this sense of ownership, those who advocate continuing the struggle will be seen by fellow Palestinians as putting their own state in jeopardy. If, however, Israel commits itself publicly to a demilitarized Palestinian state, it need not yield an inch of land until the demilitarization is firmly in place.

Israel Is in Deep Jeopardy

Americans, particularly American Jews, have an extraordinary historical responsibility at this moment. The path of least resistance—privately criticizing Israel but publicly supporting it or remaining silent—is actually a dramatic betrayal of the interests of our people. Americans must use every possible means to convey to Israelis—in private communications, in letters to Israeli newspapers and to members of Knesset, in petitions to the government of Israel, in public rallies and teach-ins, and in statements issued by synagogues and communal organizations—that Israel is in deep jeopardy and that the occupation must end.

"Americans must use every possible means to convey to Israelis . . . that Israel is in deep jeopardy and that the occupation must end."

What we do now actually may make a significant difference. Israeli centrists are under the illusion that American economic and political support can be taken for granted. Conservative leaders from the American Jewish world have fostered this fantasy. Many of these centrists can be moved to support peace proposals if they are made aware of the precariousness of their position. The ordinary Israeli has no idea how deep American disaffection has become or how such disaffection may threaten

Israel's military security in the future. The only way s/he will "get it" is through a combination of public protests and private communications. Since we can't count on Jewish leaders to convey this sense of urgency, we need to do it ourselves.

Many American Jewish leaders have displayed shortsightedness and cowardice in dealing with the current difficulties. Little in their past style of operation or in their intellectual approach gives them the tools necessary to provide leadership now that it is needed most. The neo-cons, the "Israel is always right" crowd, the people with moral blinders—none of these people can provide an analysis or a strategy that will speak to the American Jewish public. A very large number of American Jews are in a state of deep personal crisis. Their identification with Judaism, Israel, and the Jewish people is being fundamentally challenged. This is the moment when they need to hear a different kind of voice from the Jewish world. Let them hear your voice.

The crisis in Israel is a moment of truth for all of us. It should be responded to with the deepest seriousness and with the full understanding that the choices we make now may have consequences that reverberate for centuries to come.

Michael Lerner is the editor of Tikkun, *a bimonthly Jewish critique of politics, culture, and society.*

"There should be no political concessions to rioting."

Israel Should Not Withdraw from the West Bank

Charles Krauthammer

Jews are in panic. Nightly television pictures from the occupied territories have caused extraordinary unease among American Jews. In my experience, there has never been anything like it, not even during the Lebanon war. There was perhaps a higher level of anxiety in May 1967, but it was of a different kind. Then there was a sense of fear and helplessness. Now it is a feeling of taint, of corruption. Identification with the Zionist enterprise has become a source of anxiety and shame.

The situation has elicited two reactions. The first is "Not me": public dissociation from Israel's actions. The extreme, almost parodic, example of the genre was provided by Woody Allen on the op-ed page of the *New York Times*. But almost daily the letters page features yet another declaration from the famous and not so famous condemning what is going on [in] the West Bank and Gaza. This act of distancing passes for moral courage, as if there is risk for an American to come out against Israel's universally denounced policy of beatings and deportations.

It is one thing for American Jews to direct a protest at Israel. It is important for Israelis to know that diaspora Jewry will not support a policy of deliberate brutality, whatever the provocation. But it is quite another thing when the protests are designed for the American press and aimed at an American audience (as opposed to, say, appeals published in the Hebrew press or communicated directly to Israeli leaders). That serves less to sway Israeli opinion than discreetly to acquit American Jews of guilt for Israel's repressive policies. Woody Allen was writing not to move Shamir or Rabin. He was trying to reassure his tablemates at Elaine's: Not me.

Charles Krauthammer, "No Exit," *The New Republic*, March 14, 1988. Reprinted by permission of THE NEW REPUBLIC, © 1988, The New Republic, Inc.

Who asked? In times of triumph, say, the Six-Day War or Entebbe, diaspora Jews quite bask in their association with Israel. Israel has transformed the self-image and lifted the self-esteem of Jews everywhere, all the way to Moscow. But now that Israel is in crisis—caught in the vortex of an occupation it never sought and sees no safe way of ending—Israel has suddenly become alien and other. No one shunned association with Otto Preminger's Israel. Peter Jennings's Israel is another matter. Repression? Not me.

Do Something

At its most self-indulgent, "not me" is merely a public protestation of personal innocence. At its most serious, it is an expression of intolerable anguish about what is happening in Israel and to Israel. Hence the second response to moral panic that has seized American Jewry: "Do something."

Do something, do anything. This demand is addressed to Israel, though sometimes the more desperate, hoping for an imposed solution, address it to the State Department. (Desperate, because though the United States can impose on Israel, its record of imposing on Arabs is hardly encouraging.) The demand comes wrapped in the following case: The situation is intolerable—for Palestinians, for Israelis, for Americans forced to watch the wretched spectacle on television. It must stop. We know you Israelis are awaiting a negotiating partner who will recognize your existence. But there is no such partner. Israel—because it is stronger, at fault, heir to a higher moral tradition (pick one depending on your ideology)—must act first. Do something to break the impasse. This is the view, it might be noted, not just of anguished American Jews, but of such professed friends of Israel as Zbigniew Brzezinski, not previously known for excessive sensitivity to the moral dimension of foreign policy, now moved to offer Israel advice on how best, through unilateral concession, to preserve its moral standing in the world.

The situation in Israel is very bad, perhaps worse than it has ever been. But this does not mean that it could not become worse yet. Indeed, it takes no great mental effort to imagine how much worse things could be. All proposals for action, whether unilateral, bilateral, or multilateral, must therefore be examined coldly to see where they lead. If they can be reasonably shown to lead to a better situation, they should be pursued. If they cannot be shown to make things better, and most likely will make things worse, resort to them is folly, a sign, pure and simple, of a loss of nerve.

"Well, then, say the panicked, withdraw anyway and let the local radicals and/or PLO take over. . . . This is armchair strategy at its worst—facile, irresponsible, and reckless."

What, then, are the alternatives? There is really only one, though it has its variations: end the occupation, leave the territories. There are several ways of leaving: unilateral autonomy, unilateral withdrawal, international conference, negotiation with the PLO [Palestine Liberation Organization] for a PLO state. The mechanisms are different but they all have one essential feature. They involve turning the territories over to Arab control. They differ only as to the nature of that Arab control. One can talk about unilateral steps or multilateral negotiations all one wants. But the ultimate question is this: At the end of the day, when Israel leaves, who will police Nablus [a city in the West bank that was in Jordanian hands before the 1967 ceasefire]? There are only three possible candidates: 1) the young radicals whose committees are now running the "uprising," 2) the PLO and associates, or 3) the Jordanian army.

The Problem with Autonomy

Note that even the least radical Israeli step—unilateral autonomy—means turning the territories over to an Arab authority. Autonomy that amounts to Palestinians acquiring the right to collect their own garbage has already been offered and already rejected. The only autonomy that has meaning and that can affect the course of events in the territories is autonomy that includes real police power.

Who will have it? If power devolves upon the young Islamic and PLO-oriented radicals leading the demonstrations, one certain consequence will be the silencing—either by murder or intimidation—of those Palestinians the radicals call collaborationists and

Westerners call moderates. However difficult it now is for Palestinians to call for real coexistence with a Jewish state, it will be infinitely more difficult when the radicals, whose ambitions do not stop at the 1967 lines, have a monopoly of power. Moreover, even if their ambitions were so circumscribed, there is not the slightest chance that they could or would keep the PLO out of the territories. Indeed, as Glenn Frankel of the *Washington Post* and others report, the PLO has already taken operational control of what began as a spontaneous revolt. And the PLO's raison d'être is not a rump state on the West Bank—when the PLO was founded in 1964, "occupied territory" was Haifa, not Hebron—but the liberation, i.e., eradication, of pre-1967 Israel.

In practice, therefore, the first two options collapse into one. If Israel withdraws unilaterally, control of the territories falls to the PLO, though it might initially be administered through a front of local extremists. In either case, the consequences for Israel are catastrophic. Henry Kissinger is no Jewish irredentist, nor is he sentimentally attached to Judea and Samaria. But he cites the only apt historical analogy for Israel giving the territories to the PLO: Czechoslovakia after Munich, a non-viable state infiltrated at its heart by a radical and implacable enemy whose goal is annihilation.

Jordan is the only candidate for policing Nablus whose ambitions do not automatically ensure constant and intensified war with Israel. The half of the Israeli electorate that wants to give up the territories wants to give them to Jordan for precisely that reason. The problem with this solution is that even if it were possible (which is to assume improbably that King Hussein will show more courage regarding the West Bank after the rioting than before), it is irrelevant to the problem. Palestinian unrest derives ultimately from frustrated Palestinian nationalism, for which the promise of Hashemite rule is no solution at all.

A Poor Strategy

Well, then, say the panicked, withdraw anyway and let the local radicals and/or PLO take over. If things turn out badly Israel can always go back and reoccupy the territories. This is armchair strategy at its worst—facile, irresponsible, and reckless. Apart from the diplomatic, political, and sheer human costs (how many will die in that operation?), one does not undo history so easily. There is an enormous difference between putting down riots and occupying a PLO state. The PLO will have guns, not stones. What is now civil unrest will be savage civil war. If you invite Fatahland onto the West Bank, you should expect Beirut in Jerusalem. Israel fought one Lebanon war. It does not need another, fought this time within artillery range of Israel's heartland.

However wrenching the current situation, the first responsibility of a statesman is to keep his head.

And the first responsibility of Israel's friends is to consider consequences. There is no quick solution to the rioting. All the unilateral steps advocated threaten to make things much worse. No one wants tragedy, but tragedy is still preferable to catastrophe. Over two millennia Jews have acquired a tragic sense of history. But in the panic, that tradition is being challenged, indeed overwhelmed, by a contending apocalyptic, messianic tendency commanding immediate action at any cost.

The logic of Israel's current occupation of the West Bank and Gaza is the following: If Israel is to give up territory, it must get something in return. If it flees in panic, it gets nothing. What Israel gets must be peace. And that peace must be secure. Thus there are three requirements for any Israeli action regarding the territories. 1) There must exist an Arab negotiating partner. 2) That partner must offer recognition and peace and be willing to say that whatever settlement is reached marks the end of the Arab-Israeli wars. And 3) that Arab partner must be willing to take responsibility for control of the territories and not merely serve as cover or conduit for control by a party that rejects Israel's existence and seeks control of the West Bank as a first stage in an endless war on Zionism.

So long as these conditions do not exist, Israel has no choice but to patrol Nablus. For Israel to give up the territories in the absence of these conditions is to collaborate in its own destruction. Israel might take steps to encourage these conditions. History, however, does not make one sanguine about the prospect of Jews doing much to attenuate the desire of others to destroy them. But we do have one encouraging and instructive counterexample: Egypt. The lesson of Camp David is that Israel did not win recognition and peace with its unilateral withdrawal from Sinai in 1957, which was backed by wholly illusory "guarantees" from the great powers. It won recognition and peace after four lost wars convinced Egypt that Israel was a fact, and after Israel conceded territories, but only in return for contractual peace.

The Worst Possible Response

The worst possible response to the unrest is unilateral withdrawal, under whatever guise. Israel should declare its willingness to consider ceding some territory to any Arab authority that meets the (above) conditions necessary for Israel's peace and security. That authority might ultimately consist of a local West Bank leadership willing to deal with Israel. Might: such a solution must await the emergence of a Palestinian nationalism that renounces irredentism. It could be a long wait, a wait of generations.

Which brings us to the question of timing. Even if unilateral steps were not inherently dangerous, this is not the time to take them. There should be no political concessions to rioting. Whatever sympathy Israelis might have with the underlying grievance of the Palestinians, it is an elementary principle of self-preservation not to reward rioting. When rioting meets its echo, it intensifies. The Palestinians have been quite open about this. Look at what we have achieved, they say: U.S. condemnation of Israel in the U.N.; a new peace plan; a visit by Assistant Secretary of State Richard Murphy, then Secretary of State George Shultz; doubts and criticism from American Jews; dissension in Israel. If this is what we can achieve in two months of rioting, why not six months of rioting? In six months, we will get back the West Bank. In a year, all of Palestine.

Israel's response must be: Rioting gets you nothing. The absence of rioting might—we are prepared to negotiate the question—get you much. The rioting has made its point. The communication of visceral hate, the message that Israeli dreams of annexation and integrated coexistence are just dreams, is duly received. But we will not run. We will not give in to stones and strikes. Stop the rioting and we will discuss the terms of our separation.

But, say the panicked, you are missing the point. These are tired formulae. The deeper issue is that Israel is now, finally, face to face with Palestinian nationalism. Israel has met its fate and there is no escape. Israel must act.

"So long as Palestinian nationalism defines itself as contradictory to and mutually exclusive of Jewish nationalism, Israelis have no choice but to resist."

The reality of Palestinian nationalism does not escape me. What does escape me is why that reality should compel capitulation. Face to face with any threat, the first obligation is not to lose one's head. So long as Palestinian nationalism defines itself as contradictory to and mutually exclusive of Jewish nationalism, Israelis have no choice but to resist. If the game is zero sum, Jews ought not to invite a solution that leaves them with zero. So long as Palestinians, both within and without the territories, insist that history must choose between these two nationalisms, Israelis must insist that history choose Jewish nationalism—or they should pack up and, as the PLO suggests, go back to Poland.

Negotiation and compromise can only take place with a Palestinian nationalism that is prepared to accommodate its Jewish counterpart. If it is not, then there is nothing to talk about. And one does not encourage that kind of accommodative Palestinian nationalism by flight in the face of rioting, bad publicity in the West, and a case of nerves among American Jews.

There are three consequences of a precipitate Israeli withdrawal and capitulation to PLO control of the territories. The first and most obvious is the danger of unrelenting war from a well-armed, territorially based, internationally backed, irredentist PLO. A second, more subtle effect would be to mortgage Israel's security to the good will and indulgence of an enemy that has its finger on Israel's lifeline. By contracting to indefensible borders controlled by a hostile force, Israel would enter a period in which its survival depended less on its own strength than on its capacity to propitiate the enemy. This kind of dependency, all too well known to diaspora Jewry, is precisely what the Jewish state was meant to abolish.

Most ominously, and most immediately, a precipitate withdrawal from the territories would threaten Israel in an entirely different way: civil war. Israelis are bitterly and almost equally divided on how to deal with the territories. Each side believes that the other is threatening Israel's very existence with its policies. If Israel is forced prematurely to make a choice between the parties in a situation in which, unlike Camp David, there is no quid pro quo for withdrawal and no real partner for peace, there would be massive resistance within. Jews shooting at Jews has not happened in 40 years, but it did happen during the [1948-1949] War of Independence. One of Israel's great achievements has been the integration of the various armed and antagonistic Zionist tendencies into a democratic process. But more than democracy, civil peace itself would be threatened by capitulation in the territories. Endless guerrilla war from a PLO state is one route to the destruction of Israel; a quicker route is internecine warfare. It is not unimaginable. Those ready with radical and grandiose solutions for Israel's present problems should tread cautiously before demanding that Israel expose itself not only to the wrath of its enemies, but to the full fury of its own contradictions.

"It is mere escapism to believe that unilateral autonomy or unilateral withdrawal or a PLO state will rid Israel of the Palestinian issue."

There is a desperate yearning among American Jews to solve the Palestinian problem now. That yearning comes from two sources. For some, justice is the Jewish vocation. The newest liberal Jewish magazine engraves that idea in its name: *Tikkun*, from the phrase *"tikkun olam"* in Jewish liturgy

which means, literally, fixing the world. This strain of universalist Jewish utopianism is as touching as it is, for the generation after Auschwitz, anachronistic. A more persuasive case is made by realists, whose motive for redeeming the Palestinians is primarily self-regarding: only by ridding itself of the Palestinian problem will Israel save itself, body and soul. Fine. That is a solid premise for making policy. But the policy must withstand analysis. Israel will not be rid of the problem so easily. It is mere escapism to believe that unilateral autonomy or unilateral withdrawal or a PLO state will rid Israel of the Palestinian issue. In fact, it will turn *Israel* into the Palestinian issue. The question will then not be who rules Nablus. It will be who rules Haifa.

No Exit

The situation is no exit. Ultimately the best solution would be a Jordanian option, but the prospects of that happening, of either Hussein having the courage to do it or the local Palestinians having the will to accept it, are small and diminishing. The more realistic solution is for a new generation of leadership to arise in the West Bank and Gaza, which is prepared to defy the PLO and to come to an accommodation with Israel in which both nationalisms are recognized and the Hundred Years' War is declared over. Such a solution holds out the only hope for a real peace, but today that kind of Palestinian leadership is utterly lacking.

Do something. Those who demand that a solution be forced when the minimal conditions are absent are proposing to risk Jewish history to satisfy their impatience and relieve the anguish of the moment. It is a great risk to take, or, more accurately, to impose on others: American Jewry risks only discomfort and disapproval; Israel risks its survival. The conditions—the partners—are not there. Israel might do what it can to encourage their emergence, but alone it does not have the power to create them. Alone Israel has only the power to surrender.

Charles Krauthammer is a senior editor at The New Republic, *a weekly magazine.*

US Policy in the Persian Gulf Is Sensible

Richard W. Murphy

Editor's note: The following statement was delivered by Richard W. Murphy before both the Senate Foreign Relations Committee and the Subcommittee on Europe and the Middle East of the House Foreign Affairs Committee.

This [Reagan] Administration, like its predecessors, regards the [Persian] gulf as an area of major interest to the United States and is committed to maintaining the free flow of oil through the Strait of Hormuz. Consistent with our national heritage, it attaches great importance to the principle of freedom of navigation. The Administration is also firmly committed as a matter of national policy to support the individual and collective self-defense of the Arab gulf states. These longstanding U.S. undertakings flow from the strategic, economic, and political importance of the region to us.

The President has reaffirmed the direction of our long-term policy. Given the increasing dangers in the war, with its accompanying violence in the gulf, we have taken a series of specific decisions designed to ensure our strategic position in the gulf and reassert the fundamental U.S. stabilizing role. Frankly, in the light of the Iran-*Contra* revelations, we had found that the leaders of the gulf states were questioning the coherence and seriousness of U.S. policy in the gulf along with our reliability and staying power. We wanted to be sure the countries with which we have friendly relations—Iraq and GCC [Gulf Cooperation Council] states—as well as the Soviet Union and Iran understood the firmness of our commitments. On January 23 and again on February 25 [1987], President Reagan issued statements reiterating our commitment to the flow of oil through the strait and U.S. support for the self-defense effort of the gulf states. He also endorsed Operation Staunch, our

Richard W. Murphy, "International Shipping and the Iran-Iraq War," delivered before the Senate Foreign Relations Committee and the Subcommittee on Europe and the Middle East of the House Foreign Affairs Committee, United States Department of State, *Current Policy,* No. 958.

effort to reduce the flow of weapons from others to Iran.

While neutral toward the Iran-Iraq war, the U.S. Government views the continuation of this conflict, as well as its potential expansion, as a direct threat to our interests. We are working intensively for the earliest possible end to the conflict, with the territorial integrity and independence of both sides intact. As the President asserted in his February 25 statement on the war, we believe that "the time to act on this dangerous and destructive war is now." He urged an intensified international effort to seek an end to the war, and we have taken a lead in UN Security Council (UNSC) consultations to achieve this aim. As we announced May 7 [1987], the United States is "ready in principle to support the application of appropriate enforcement measures against either party which refuses to cooperate with formal UNSC efforts to end the war."

An International Consensus

While there remains much work to be done in New York, I believe that an international consensus is growing that this war has gone on too long—the suffering of the Iraqi and Iranian peoples has been too great—and the threat to international interests is so direct that more active measures are required. As you know, Iraq has long shown its willingness to end the fighting; Iran remains recalcitrant.

Operation Staunch has been pursued in recent months with new vigor. I believe its effectiveness has not been seriously impaired, as many expected, by the Iran revelations.

In addition to the inherent tragedy and suffering in Iraq and Iran, as the fighting drags on, with mounting casualties and drains on the economies of these two nations, so grows the threat of the war spilling over to nearby friendly states in the gulf. The fresh threats to international shipping are one example of such spillover effect.

Attacks on neutral shipping passing through the Strait of Hormuz have increased in intensity. A total of nearly 100 vessels were hit by Iran and Iraq in 1986; in the first 3 months of [1987], some 30 ships were attacked, including a Soviet merchant ship. [Between May 1 and May 19, 1987, Iran] attacked 5 ships of nonbelligerent countries, virtually all in commerce with Kuwait. Attacks now occur at night as well as day, by sea as well as air, by small boats armed with light weapons as well as by helicopters launched from Iranian warships. While Iran has yet to sink a ship, most of those attacked have suffered damage, some seriously, and innocent lives have been lost.

Attack on the USS *Stark*

The May 17 [1987] attack on the U.S.S. *Stark* was the first attack on a U.S. warship in the war. This tragic accident gives emphasis to our caution to both belligerents that the war in the gulf could lead to mistakes and miscalculations; it must be ended.

We have increased the state of alert of U.S. Navy ships in the gulf and warned belligerent states (i.e., Iran and Iraq) that our ships will fire if one of their aircraft should approach in a manner indicating possible hostile intent—as did the Iraqi F-1 which attacked the U.S.S. *Stark*.

"Consistent with longstanding U.S. commitment to the flow of oil through the gulf . . . the President decided that the United States would help in the protection of Kuwaiti tankers."

The Chinese delivery to and testing by Iran of Chinese Silkworm antiship missiles at the Strait of Hormuz present a potentially serious threat to U.S. and other shipping. With their 85-kilometer range and 1,100-pound warhead, these missiles can span the strait at its narrowest point and represent, for the first time, a realistic Iranian capability to sink large oil tankers. Whatever Iran's motivation for procuring such threatening missiles, their presence gives Iran the ability both to intimidate the gulf states and gulf shippers and to cause a real or *de facto* closure of the strait. The Chinese decision to sell such weaponry to Iran is most unwelcome and disturbing. We have made clear to both Iran and China the seriousness with which we consider the Silkworm threat. Other concerned governments have done the same. It is our hope that a sustained international diplomatic campaign will convince Iran not to use the Silkworms.

Iran has been using a combination of military action, attacks on gulf shipping, and terrorism, as

well as shrewd diplomacy, to intimidate the gulf states not involved in the war. It has tried to impress upon gulf states the hopelessness of their looking to the United States for help and to divide the gulf states one from the other.

Kuwait has been a particular target of Iranian threats. While not a belligerent, Kuwait's size and location make it highly vulnerable to intimidation. The Iranian regime has inspired terrorist and sabotage incidents within Kuwait, fired missiles on Kuwaiti territory on the eve of the January [1987] Islamic summit, and attacked over 24 vessels serving Kuwaiti ports since September [1986]. . . . Over the last 3 years, Iranian-influenced groups have attempted a series of bombings and attacks, including on the ruler of Kuwait himself, in an attempt to liberate terrorists being held in Kuwait who were convicted of bombing the U.S. and French Embassies.

Helping Kuwait

Kuwait and other GCC states expressed to us their concern about the continuing attacks by Iran on tankers. Kuwait asked for our assistance, fearing potential damage to its economic lifeline. Consistent with longstanding U.S. commitment to the flow of oil through the gulf and the importance we attach to the freedom of navigation in international waters, as well as our determination to assist our friends in the gulf, the President decided that the United States would help in the protection of Kuwaiti tankers. In the context of these developments, Kuwait asked to register a number of ships in its tanker fleet under U.S. flag. We informed Kuwait that if the vessels in question met ownership and other technical requirements under U.S. laws and regulations, they could be registered under the U.S. flag. This is in accordance with our established position on qualifications for U.S. flag registration of commercial vessels in general. We also informed the Kuwaitis that by virtue of the fact that these vessels would fly the American flag, they would receive the U.S. Navy protection given any U.S. flag vessel transiting the gulf. The U.S. Navy has always had the mission to provide appropriate protection for U.S. commercial shipping worldwide within the limits of available resources and consistent with international law.

Kuwait welcomed our response, and we have together proceeded with the registry process. The Coast Guard has begun inspection of the vessels in order to determine their conformity with U.S. safety and other technical standards.

We view the reflagging of Kuwaiti tankers [by] the United States as an unusual measure to meet an extraordinary situation. It would not, however, set a precedent for the normal conduct of commercial shipping or affect the broad interests of the U.S. maritime industry. U.S. flagging procedures minimally require that only the captain of each vessel be a U.S. citizen. Because these vessels will not be calling at U.S. ports, there is no requirement that they carry U.S. seamen or other U.S. crewmembers. These new U.S. flag vessels will be sailing in areas where other U.S. flag vessels have generally not frequented since the war began.

To date, Iran has been careful to avoid confrontations with U.S. flag vessels when U.S. Navy vessels have been in the vicinity. U.S. Military Sealift Command and other commercial U.S. flag vessels have transited the gulf each month under U.S. Navy escort without incident. We believe that our naval presence will continue to have this deterrent effect. Iran lacks the sophisticated aircraft and weaponry used by Iraq in the mistaken attack on the U.S.S. *Stark*. Moreover, we will make sure in advance that Iran knows which ships have been reflagged and are under U.S. protection.

Demonstrating Our Clear Resolve

Our response to Kuwait demonstrates our resolve to protect our interests and those of our friends in the region, and it has been warmly welcomed by those governments with which we have had traditionally close ties. Our goal is to deter, not provoke; we believe this is understood by the parties in the region—including Iran. We will pursue our program steadily and with determination.

In providing this protection, our actions will be fully consistent with the applicable rules of international law, which clearly recognize the right of a neutral state to escort and protect ships flying its flag which are not carrying contraband. In this case, this includes the fact that U.S. ships will not be carrying oil from Iraq. Neither party to the conflict will have any basis for taking hostile action against U.S. naval ships or the vessels they will protect.

Our judgment is that, in light of all the surrounding circumstances, the protection accorded by U.S. naval vessels to these U.S. flag tankers transiting international waters or straits does not constitute introduction of our armed forces into a situation where "imminent involvement in hostilities is clearly indicated." The War Powers Resolution, accordingly, is not implicated by our actions. On the contrary, our actions are such as to make it clear that any prospect of hostilities is neither imminent nor clearly indicated. I repeat that our intention is to deter, not provoke, further military action. We will, however, keep the situation under careful review—particularly in light of the May 17 attack on the U.S.S. *Stark*—and keep Congress closely informed.

Kuwait has also discussed with other maritime powers commercial charter arrangements in the interest of deterring further Iranian attacks on its vessels. We understand that Kuwait broached this issue with all permanent members of the UN Security Council and has entered into an agreement with the Soviet Union to charter three long-haul, Soviet flag vessels to transport some of its oil out of the gulf.

A constant of U.S. policy for decades has been U.S. determination to prevent enhanced Soviet influence and presence in the gulf. We do not want the Soviet Union to obtain a strategic position from which it could threaten vital free-world interests in the region. We believe our arrangement with Kuwait will limit Soviet advances in the region; they would have welcomed the opportunity to replace us and used this position to try to expand further their role in the gulf. We understand that their commercial charter arrangement for long-haul charters out of the gulf does not necessitate an increase in the Soviet naval presence or establishment of facilities in the gulf. This we would not welcome and have made our position clear.

"Our policies are carefully conceived— and they focus on steps needed to end the war."

I want to be frank to acknowledge, however, that the disturbing trend in the war—its spread in geographic terms and its increasing impact on third parties like Kuwait—creates the circumstances in which the Soviets may find more opportunities to insert themselves. The U.S.S.R. plays a fundamentally different role in the gulf and is viewed by Iran as directly threatening to Tehran. Aside from the long northern border, Soviets occupy Afghanistan to Iran's east and are Iraq's primary source of arms. The unescorted Soviet ship recently attacked had, in the past, carried arms to Iraq. The Soviets sent warships into the gulf for the first time after Iran boarded and searched a Soviet arms-carrying vessel. Iran should ponder this development as it maintains its intransigent war policy. We certainly believe the Soviet actions in the gulf and their attempts to enhance their presence there further emphasize the need to bring this war to an end.

Clear and Consistent Policies

In conclusion, the Administration is following a clear and consistent set of policies in support of our national interests in the gulf. Our policies are carefully conceived—and they focus on steps needed to end the war. They are calm and steady in purpose, not provocative in intent; they should help deter Iranian miscalculations and actions that would require a strong response. By supporting the defensive efforts of the moderate gulf states, including the sale of appropriate defensive arms, we help to enable them to defend the interests we share in the gulf and to reduce the prospects for closer ties with the Soviet Union as well as any inclination to accommodate Iranian hegemony.

We want the Congress to be fully aware of what we are doing. That is why we provided, in March and April [1987], a number of briefings on our gulf policy and what we intended to do to help Kuwait, including briefings to the House Foreign Affairs Committee and Senate Foreign Relations Committee. That is why the President has, on several occasions, issued public statements explaining our policy. We have a coherent and effective policy in the gulf region. We seek your support and that of the U.S. public for our efforts. We believe it is important for the United States to work more actively to end the Iran-Iraq war, to be prepared to defend the principle of the free flow of oil and meet our long-standing commitment to assist the gulf Arab states in their self-defense, and to continue to work to constrain Soviet designs. We will advise Congress on the evolution of our discussions with Kuwait and the continuing security situation.

Richard W. Murphy is US assistant secretary for Near Eastern and South Asian Affairs.

"Our Iran policy is largely based on irrational fears or improbable predictions that encourage us to act rashly."

viewpoint 17

US Policy in the Persian Gulf Is Irrational

Nikki R. Keddie

After several years of keeping Iran at arm's length, the Reagan administration plunged into two dramatic policy initiatives: first, the ill-fated arms-for-hostages dealings; and then the Persian Gulf reflagging initiative, which began in June 1987 and shows no sign of ending in the near future. Apart from their dramatic activism, the two policies appear on the surface to be very different. The Iran arms policy was secret and carried out by a few men, while our entry into the Gulf has been highly publicized and involves large military forces. The former policy strengthened Iran, while the latter clearly benefits Iraq. Yet there are important factors common to both policies that are typical of our overall approach to the region.

The first such common element is a basic lack of understanding of revolutionary Iran, the historical and cultural forces shaping its foreign policy, and the nature of Iranian attitudes toward the West, especially our own country. The second common factor is a crude anti-Sovietism that leads officials to view events in the Gulf through the prism of East-West conflict. As a result of these misperceptions, common sense and attempts at understanding are often abandoned when U.S. policymakers discuss Iran. Instead, our Iran policy is largely based on irrational fears or improbable predictions that encourage us to act rashly.

In both these Iran initiatives, the administration rushed into ill-conceived policies without sufficiently considering how Iran might react. The Irangate affair was characterized by wishful thinking about the possibility of enlisting Iran in an anti-Soviet entente. In the Gulf initiative, the White House seriously underestimated the potential costs and risks of our actions. It was thought, for example, that the reflagging and escorting of shipping could be

accomplished using only ships we already had in the Gulf, and that the Iranians would not attack U.S. forces directly although they might undertake terrorist acts elsewhere.

This lack of forethought and understanding has been exacerbated by the eagerness of some administration officials to plunge into high-risk "macho" adventures without having heard and digested expert opinion on the possible consequences. Some of those who advocate such aggressive policies in the Gulf region believe that this foreign policy style has been vindicated by the two cases where it apparently "worked"—the invasion of Grenada and the bombing of Libya. But even if one considers these actions to have been effective, it is another matter entirely to believe that similar policies will bring Iran to heel.

US Misperceptions

Our misperceptions of the situation in Iran and the Gulf have not even had the virtue of consistency. Wildly differing estimates of Iran were given by administration officials during the two initiatives, almost none of which resembled what would have been said by most competent Iran specialists. Between 1984 and 1986, it was alternately claimed that Khomeini's Iran was on the brink of collapse, and that the Islamic Republic was powerful and important enough to merit a partial U.S.-Iranian alliance against the Soviet Union and its forces in Afghanistan. Time and again the United States pinned its hopes on uncovering the elusive "moderates" within the Iranian government. But public reaction to the Iran-contra affair ended this quest and Iran once more became a "Great Satan," intent on controlling the Gulf and the states on its border and not to be trusted about anything.

Unfortunately, the experiences of the 1979 hostage crisis and Irangate have made most Americans ready to believe anything bad about Iran; as a result,

Nikki R. Keddie, "Iranian Imbroglios: Who's Irrational?" *World Policy Journal*, Winter 1987-88. Reprinted with permission.

uninformed anti-Iranian sentiments may lead them to support policies that risk war in the Gulf. The current U.S. policy toward Iran, based on mistrust, misunderstanding, and de facto support of Iran's enemies, is unlikely to encourage fruitful negotiations on ending the Iran-Iraq war—negotiations that may take time and that will have to take account of Iran's position as well as Iraq's.

A tendency to view the Gulf through the prism of the Cold War has similarly produced policies that have set back, rather than advanced, our interests in the region. U.S. foreign policy planners assign high priority to Iran and the Gulf, and one of their greatest fears is that the Soviet Union or a pro-Soviet Iran might attempt to take control of the region and its vital oil export capacities. In recent years, however, this concern has resulted more in precipitous and ill-conceived actions than in rational planning. A prime example is our unthinking entry into the Gulf in response to the prospect of the Soviets' reflagging a few Kuwaiti ships. A rational and well-considered policy that could ultimately lead to agreements and compromises among the major parties would be much more conducive to stability in the region than our present unilateral policies, particularly since it is no longer possible for one power or group of allies to control the Gulf and adjacent states. The whole premise that the Soviets can be kept out of a region they border on, and the lack thus far of alternative policies toward the Soviets—notably trying to involve them in regional agreements—are aspects of our Gulf policy that have hardly been questioned.

> "Our misperceptions of the situation in Iran and the Gulf have not even had the virtue of consistency."

Crude anti-Sovietism and blindness to the real forces shaping Iran's foreign policy have moreover allowed us to be manipulated by others against our own interests. In the Iran-contra affair, we were exploited by Israelis and Iranian leaders alike, as well as by profiteering international arms salesmen who doubled as diplomats—men like Manuchehr Ghorbanifar, Al Schwimmer, Yacov Nimrodi, Albert Hakim, and General Richard Secord. In our Gulf policy we have allowed ourselves to be used by the Arab Gulf states—Kuwait, Iraq, and Saudi Arabia—that would like to see us fully committed to fighting Iran so that the war can be settled on terms favorable to Iraq. In both cases, self-seeking third parties have tried to make it seem that their favored policy was in America's best interest, often by invoking the communist and Soviet bogies.

Yet neither of the two policies was or is in long-term U.S. interests, even as conservatively defined. A policy of neutrality in the Iran-Iraq war, combined with patient efforts to end the conflict—efforts that must necessarily involve the Soviet Union—would be far more conducive to stability in the Gulf than a policy of helping one side, whether Iran or Iraq, to gain its own terms. Policies that favor either side are likely to continue to rebound against the United States and produce an extreme reaction in the opposite direction, as they have until now. The Iran arms sales, for example, alarmed friendly Arab states so much that they pressed us to adopt a pro-Kuwait and pro-Iraq stance once the policy was disclosed. And our entry into the Gulf has pushed Iran into a series of agreements with the Soviet Union and a much harder line toward the United States. Neither side trusts us: neither the Iranians, for reasons suggested above, nor the Iraqis, who do not want to risk breaking with the Soviets, their chief arms supplier. As of late 1987, the Soviets have more influence in the region than they have had for many years—precisely the development we had hoped to avoid. . . .

Unthinking and Dangerous

A preoccupation with Moscow's regional intentions, together with anger against Iran and a need to reassure Arab countries in the wake of the Irangate fiasco, propelled the administration into an unthinking and dangerous policy in the Gulf. Late in 1986, Kuwait, a de facto ally of Iraq, asked both the United States and the Soviet Union to reflag and escort its tankers, which Iran was attacking in retaliation for Iraqi naval attacks. Kuwait, like Iraq, had an interest in internationalizing the war by drawing in the two superpowers, since either could be expected to try to prevent an Iranian victory. The administration's decision to reflag Kuwaiti ships originated as a hasty counter to the Soviets' positive response to Kuwait's request.

Kuwait was thus able to manipulate U.S. alarm about the Soviets to its own ends of reducing or ending Iranian attacks on its ships. There were no signs that the Reagan administration appreciated the problems and dangers involved. U.S. allies were not informed or consulted before the fact, nor were Kuwaiti and other Gulf state refusals of our requests for military cooperation effectively anticipated. Mines were not foreseen or prepared for, and the U.S. government acted as if it thought, in the face of years of contrary evidence about Iranian determination, that Iran would simply fold in the face of a threatening U.S. presence. U.S. policy was clearly responding more to a desire to bring back the credibility lost in the Iran-contra affair than to any thoughtful evaluation of U.S. interests. Then came Iraq's attack on the *U.S.S. Stark* on May 17, 1987, which some think was deliberately designed to bring U.S. forces into the Gulf (though it is possible to wonder whether anyone is clever enough to foresee that openly attacking a U.S. vessel is the way to bring the United States in on your side in a war). Until the *Stark* incident, our leaders had thought the reflagging and escorting could be done without extra ships, but the attack resulted in the dispatch of a huge American armada. Predictably, tensions between Iran and the United States began to escalate.

"A preoccupation with Moscow's regional intentions . . . propelled the administration into an unthinking and dangerous policy in the Gulf."

At first glance, the rarely stressed goal of proving our bona fides to Arab states after the Irangate fiasco might appear to have been successful, as Saudi Arabia, Kuwait, and Iraq are less unhappy with us now than they were. Yet upon closer examination, the results of our policy are far less positive: the conservative Arab states are currently limiting our options by insisting that we adopt an uncompromising hard-line anti-Iranian position in the war, while at the same time they do not want us to draw them into hostilities with Iran.

An Ally of Iraq

In all but name, the United States has become an ally of Iraq. This has hardly been conducive to regional stability: violence in the Gulf has increased ever since we sent in our armada. For example, there have been numerous Iraqi attacks on Iran-bound shipping, which we have done nothing to stop, despite our repeated statements that we aim to halt the tanker war (which is an Iraqi initiative). The fact is that our presence has facilitated Iraqi attacks. Although in late 1987 there were signs that both Iran and the United States were avoiding provocations, Iraq could well decide to create an anonymous incident (such as terrorist action, or laying mines) that could bring us into direct hostilities with Iran.

Even in geostrategic terms, our de facto alliance with Iraq makes little sense. Iran is a far larger, more populous, and more important country than Iraq. There seems little doubt that our policies have encouraged Iran's growing turn to Soviet aid, economic relations, and advice in recent months, and have also encouraged the increasing ascendancy of hard-line policies within the Iranian government. Clearly, our massive compensatory tilt toward Iraq may end up damaging U.S. interests as much as the prior tilt toward Iran.

Confusion over goals has been as extreme in the Gulf as in Irangate. According to a report on U.S.

Gulf policy produced for the Senate Foreign Relations Committee in October 1987, none of the ostensible rationales of U.S. Gulf policy has worked out. In fact, we have generally achieved the opposite of what we said we wanted. The administration has offered three main rationales for its Gulf policy: ensuring the free flow of oil, defending freedom of navigation, and preventing Soviet encroachments. In fact:

• Oil supplies have never been in danger, and the world faces a glut, not a shortage, of oil. Interference with the flow of oil in the Iran-Iraq war has affected only about 1 percent of oil exports. This does not endanger U.S. imports, while the U.S. allies whom it could affect have been far more reluctant than we to send ships to the Gulf.

A constantly increasing percentage of Gulf-produced oil is moved by pipeline, including all Iraqi and much Saudi oil, which makes the Gulf less crucial to the world's oil supply than it used to be. The presence of underutilized sources of oil far from the Gulf area has a similar effect. Although Gulf oil may become more crucial in the future, it is also probable that the shift to pipelines instead of tankers in the area will continue.

• With regard to freedom of navigation, so few of the Gulf's total ships are protected that at best the U.S. presence could have only a minimally positive effect on Gulf shipping. It does affect shipping negatively, however, since the Iranians now feel called upon to be far more active than before and Iraq has likewise stepped up its anti-Iranian attacks. Shipping has thus become riskier than ever, as some predicted it would.

Iraq Started the Naval War

Iran's activity in the Gulf before the U.S. entry was almost entirely in retaliation for Iraqi attacks on tankers bound for Iran; the Iranians are the party most interested in keeping the Gulf open to tankers. It has been Iraq, not Iran, that over the years has attacked and disrupted by far the most shipping, for the simple reason that Iran depends completely on the Gulf and the Strait of Hormuz to export all its oil, while Iraq sends its oil abroad by pipeline. The United States could do far more to pacify the Gulf, if that is what it really wants to do, by persuading Iraq to stop its attacks on Iranian shipping, which are what started and perpetuate the naval war in the Gulf. Naturally the Iraqis are not going to want to do this without some major moves toward settlement of the war.

• The prospects for Soviet advances are limited by the wariness with which most states in the region regard the Soviets. Nevertheless, U.S. Gulf policy has backfired in that it has clearly increased Soviet influence in Iran—by far the most important country in the region. In recent months Iranian and Soviet leaders have been conferring more frequently, and in the all-important Teheran Friday sermons, as well as in other Iranian public statements, denunciations of the Soviets have been replaced with compliments. If the revelations of Irangate tended to push Iran toward better relations with the Soviet Union, our actions in the Gulf do so even more. . . .

Counterproductive Policy

Quite clearly, then, U.S. policy toward Iran has proved counterproductive. It has also made the settlement of the Gulf War—another ostensible goal of U.S. policy—more difficult. Before our intervention, some progress toward resolution could be noted in U.N.-sponsored efforts, especially those of the secretary general. But rather than promote that trend, America's unilateral use of force in the Gulf has encouraged the two warring countries to embrace more hard-line positions. Iraq, emboldened by U.S. tacit support, now feels it can afford to hang tough, while Iran resists compromise so as not to seem to be yielding to pressures from the Great Satan. . . .

"Quite clearly, . . . U.S. policy toward Iran has proved counterproductive."

If hard work and patience in the hope of an eventual result seem to be the best counsel now, we may take some encouragement from the recent improvement in U.S.-Soviet relations. Certainly there is far more hope for a settlement of the Iran-Iraq war and related questions if the United States and the Soviet Union work together than if they work against each other. This is likely to require some compromise with Soviet positions. From the problems created by our precipitous leap into the Gulf we may finally learn that it is easier to scramble eggs than to unscramble them, and that in the future we should therefore act with much more caution and a more informed and realistic view of dangerous situations.

Nikki R. Keddie is professor of history at the University of California at Los Angeles and the author of Roots of Revolution: An Interpretive History of Modern Iran.

viewpoint **18**

The US Should Support Iraq

Frederick W. Axelgard

"Should the United States be taking Iraq's side in the Gulf war?" During 1987, this question has gained currency as a mechanism for criticizing U.S. military and diplomatic initiatives relating to the Persian Gulf. Like most rhetorical ploys, this query glosses over facts and incorporates hidden assumptions to facilitate arrival at a predetermined point—in this case, to argue that the United States really has no business deploying men and equipment in the dangerous setting of the Gulf.

But *has* the United States taken Iraq's side in its war with Iran? And is it automatically wrong for the United States to identify with Iraqi interests and objectives? The conventional wisdom that underpins most criticism of current U.S. policy in the Gulf would answer both questions with a firm "yes." In both cases, though, this answer would be wrong, as a closer examination of the complex realities in the Gulf will show.

A Distorted Perspective

The prevailing American and international perspective on the Iran-Iraq war is hopelessly distorted. It is preoccupied with Iraqi and Iranian attacks on maritime targets in the Gulf and the formidable Western naval presence deployed to contain the effects of this so-called tanker war. But the war between Iran and Iraq is first and last a ground war. The offshore conflict is but a sideshow against what has happened (and surely will yet happen) onshore. More than seven years of bloody offensives, counteroffensives, bombings, and missile attacks have resulted in upwards of one million casualties and damages totaling hundreds of billions of dollars for the two sides. This horrific fallout completely overshadows the losses incurred in the four-year-old tanker war. Furthermore, it is a

foregone conclusion that the course of the war and its ultimate resolution will be determined by facts on the ground, not in the water.

With these points in mind, two observations are in order about U.S. policy toward the war. First, its thrust has been to contain the *international* repercussions of the war, and it has had relatively little direct effect on the ground war. The deployment of naval forces in the Gulf is a perfect example of this practice. Second, to the degree Washington has had an effect on the ground war, the net results have almost certainly been more to Iran's benefit rather than Iraq's. Moreover, a strong argument can also be made that Iran has received more immediate and concrete benefits from the presence of Western naval forces in the Gulf than has Iraq.

The core argument here is that the impetus given to Iran's basic war effort by the secret, U.S.-sanctioned arms sales of 1985-86 far surpasses the positive effect of anything America has done for Iraq in terms of military, diplomatic, or economic support. To begin with, one must challenge the administration's *de minimus* assessment of the amount of arms it sold to Iran. It claimed that the TOW antitank missiles and Hawk air-defense equipment sent to Iran were valued at about $12 million and could fit in one planeload. The lengthy congressional investigations of the Iran arms scandal never examined this claim seriously in public, perhaps out of fear that it would create more political difficulty for Israel. But one experienced observer, former National Security Council official Gary Sick, has estimated that Iran received between $500 million and $1 billion in arms from Israel and the United States in 1985-86, a factor of 50 to 100 times greater than the administration's claims.

Congress and the mainstream American press have also judiciously avoided another potentially critical question: What added amounts of weaponry have

Frederick W. Axelgard, "U.S. Policy in the Gulf: A Second Look." This article appeared in the December 1987 issue and is reprinted with permission from *The World & I*, a publication of the Washington Times Corporation. Copyright 1987.

gotten through to Tehran from various arms suppliers around the world because of the "green light" given by the U.S. sales? The credibility of the well-publicized "Operation Staunch," the U.S. campaign begun in 1984 to dissuade Western countries from supplying arms to Iran, was clearly undermined by the Iran arms scandal. As a result, it is highly probable that once-reluctant suppliers resumed sales to Iran in recent months, particularly after the expansion of Iranian oil exports in the spring of 1987.

There are also qualitative grounds for skepticism about the official assertion that the arms sales to Iran did not affect the balance in the Iran-Iraq war. Analyses of the fighting around the Iraqi city of Basra in January 1987 showed Iran had markedly improved in antitank warfare and air-defense capability, developments that some observers ascribed to the antitank and antiaircraft weapons Iran had acquired from the United States. But Reagan administration officials were not fazed by the coincidence of the arms sales and Iran's increased effectiveness and have repeatedly denied that there was any connection between the two.

"Iraq has received no weapons from the United States, let alone any that have direct applicability to the ground war."

But to focus on ramifications affecting the numerical and technological balance in the war overlooks that it is the *psychological* balance that has been the paramount concern in the Iran-Iraq conflict for several years now. Iran has long been outgunned by Iraq in every aspect of its arsenal except raw manpower. Yet, it is Iranian forces that have seized and held the initiative and have made threatening penetrations into Iraq in each of the past four years. Indeed, the political and psychological impact of seeing the U.S. superpower reduced to selling arms clandestinely to Khomeini's Iran is probably the most critical blow dealt by the entire episode. In this way, the U.S arms sales added decisively to Iran's existing advantage in a key determinant of the future of the ground war. In the short term, they certainly helped incite Iran to make its deepest penetration yet, toward Basra in the beginning of 1987. Only time will tell what their long-term consequences will be.

No Weapons to Iraq

And what of the effectiveness of U.S. assistance to Iraq? To begin with, it must be underscored that by all known accounts, Iraq has received no weapons from the United States, let alone any that have direct applicability to the ground war like the antitank

missiles and air-defense enhancements shipped to Iran. This stark discrepancy in Iraq's status was reemphasized in the aftermath of Iran-gate, when Washington rejected a request for Iraq to obtain military transport planes and the use of a defensive artillery radar system.

The main assistance Iraq *has* received from the United States consists of some $3 billion in agricultural credits, military intelligence information, and, only recently, active diplomacy and naval involvement in the Gulf to pressure Iran to end the war. Overall, Iraq appears to have received far less direct U.S. assistance in its war effort than Iran has.

US Intelligence Connection

The agricultural credits, for example, while appreciated by Iraq, have not had an appreciable direct impact on the war. More important, however, has been the U.S. intelligence data Iraq has reportedly received since U.S.-Iraqi diplomatic relations were restored in late 1984. The military significance of this information—which has reportedly consisted mainly of satellite photographs showing Iranian troop movements and artillery placements—was never subjected to public scrutiny, although it was assumed to be an unqualified benefit to Iraq's defensive war effort.

This assumption began to erode early in 1987, when press reports stemming from the Iran arms scandal quoted U.S. officials as saying that misleading intelligence had been passed to both Iraq and Iran. Soon afterward, Iraq's first deputy premier, Taha Yassin Ramadhan, made a public charge that Washington had deliberately falsified intelligence it gave to Iraq just prior to Iran's Fao offensive in February 1986. This surprise attack was a grave military and psychological setback for Iraq because Iran occupied a sizable part of the Fao peninsula and killed several thousand Iraqi soldiers. U.S. officials denied having deliberately misled Iraq, but it soon became clear that U.S. intelligence had nevertheless "missed the call" by drawing attention to Iranian strength in the central battle sector, far north of Fao.

In summary, it appears that even after discounting Iraq's charges of deliberate fraud, the possibility remains that U.S. intelligence diverted Iraqi attention from Fao and thereby might have contributed to Iraq's most damaging setback in the war since 1982. At the very least, this was Iraq's perception of matters, and it clearly cast a cloud of uncertainty on the reliability and usefulness of the U.S. intelligence connection. Hence, one could hardly argue that U.S. intelligence aid to Iraq effectively offsets the damage done by U.S. arms sales to Iran.

There are similar problems with the argument that Iraq has been a significant beneficiary of recent U.S. diplomatic and military initiatives supposedly designed to put pressure on Iran. In fact, the most immediate and concrete consequences of these initiatives have been seriously detrimental to Iraq. The July 20 [1987] cease-fire order passed unanimously by the UN Security Council as Resolution 598 resulted from UN consultations begun by U.S. diplomats during the disturbing Iranian ground advances in early 1987. But because it took effect at a time when Iranian ground offensives were not "in season," the resolution's first and most direct impact was to focus pressure on Iraqi attacks on Iranian targets in the Gulf.

This de facto segmentation of the cease-fire order exactly contradicted Iraq's insistence that pressure be brought to bear to end fighting on all fronts, not just offshore. Predictably, Iraq refused to be bound permanently by this arrangement and, in late August [1987], it resumed attacks in the gulf after a six-week pause. This action eroded the international perception of Iraq as the victim of Iran's intransigence, a muddying of the diplomatic waters that certainly did not serve Baghdad's interest. Indeed, it contributed to the postponement of follow-up action by the Security Council in the form of an arms embargo sanction against Iran, the only measure on the diplomatic horizon that promises direct, tangible benefits for Iraq.

Nor could Iraq be pleased with the fact that the presence of U.S. and Western naval forces in the Gulf provided a shield behind which Iran markedly expanded its oil exports. The intensity of Iraq's air war in the Gulf perceptibly declined immediately after the tragic bombing of the USS *Stark* in May [1987]. This pattern was reinforced during the 40-day "lull" that followed passage of Resolution 598. Iran, meanwhile, took advantage of the situation to jack up its oil exports to the highest levels in years, in excess of two million barrels per day. As if this irony were insufficient, it has since been shown that the United States became perhaps the largest purchaser of these extra Iranian oil exports, providing Tehran with more than $350 [million] in revenues in July 1987 alone.

Time for Reexamination

The above discussion provides ample reason to reexamine the assertion that the United States has effectively taken Iraq's side in the Gulf war. Those Reagan administration initiatives designed to help Iraq and/or pressure Iran have either been substantially compromised or have had the opposite effect. This will not disappoint a goodly segment of observers of U.S. Middle East policy—namely, those for whom any close ties at all to Iraq are anathema.

For most of the postwar era, U.S.-Iraqi relations have been tense and only marginally important to America's main regional interests. Iraq broke off relations during the June 1967 war to protest U.S. support for Israel and did not restore ties until November 1984, long after other Arab states had done so. This extreme action, by a country that is

not even on the front line in the Arab-Israeli conflict, is indicative of the vehement attitude that both pre- and postrevolutionary Iraqi regimes have had toward the Arab-Israeli dispute. It also suggests why successive U.S. administrations have not viewed Iraq as a focus of serious, constructive policy interest.

U.S. policymakers have also been put off by Iraq's 1972 treaty of friendship and alliance with the Soviet Union; its active opposition to the Camp David accords; its image as a perennially unstable polity; and by its opposition to U.S. attempts in the 1970s to build a policy in the Gulf around the "twin pillars" of the shah's Iran and Saudi Arabia.

The legacy left by these factors—and almost instinctive disbelief that Washington and Baghdad could ever have a serious policy interest in common—is another cause of criticism of the Reagan administration's policy in the Gulf. But this criticism, too, is ill-founded, since it depends on an outdated assessment of Iraq and the circumstances affecting U.S. interests in the Gulf.

Changes in Iraq

Most close watchers of Iraq agree that the country is in the midst of monumental change. Many observers attribute this change—affecting both domestic politics and foreign policy—solely to the pressure induced by the war with Iran. In fact, though, almost every aspect of Iraq's wartime transformation can be traced to significant adjustments begun in the 1970s. These include the political stabilization of the state under the leadership of Sadam Hussein and the Baath party; Iraq's emergence as a major actor in the international oil market; a decline in Iraqi-Soviet ties and the expansion of political and economic relations with the West; and closer ties between Iraq and the conservative Arab states of the Gulf, particularly after Ayatollah Khomeini's victory in Iran.

"It is of long-term importance for Western countries, including the United States, to keep an opening with Iraq."

The major change of concern to U.S. interests is, of course, Iraq's importance as a barrier to the expansion of Iran's Islamic revolution. Since about 1983, Washington has held as a policy position the belief that Iraq's survival against Iran's military onslaught is vital. Thus, after many years of either being tangential or hostile to major U.S. policy objectives in the Middle East, Iraq now has central significance.

But gainsayers eager to minimize Iraq's importance argue that it is negatively premised and temporary at best. Once Khomeini dies, they reason, the threat to Iraq will vanish and Iran will reemerge as the strategic "prize" in the Gulf. But this logic would seem to rest on two debatable predictions: that Iran's leadership after Khomeini will not be stridently Islamic and that Iranian-Iraqi hostility will die out soon after Khomeini's demise. If either prediction fails, the strategic regional balance between Iraq and Iran will remain at risk, and the need for Western help to maintain this balance will persist. In short, it is of long-term importance for Western countries, including the United States, to keep an opening with Iraq.

Iran or Iraq?

The assertion that Iran will reemerge as the strategic prize in the Gulf also bears closer examination. Does it imply that future relations with Iran will be so important that they render relations with Gulf powers like Iraq irrelevant? If so, this assertion negates two fundamental lessons driven home by the experience of the last 10 years: The first is that America's monolithic dependence on the shah to protect its Gulf interests was self-deceptive and self-defeating; the second is that no future leader of Iran will soon embrace the United States as completely as did the shah. In other words, Washington cannot go back and reclaim an exclusive strategic relationship with Iran as its Gulf policy, and it should not even want to.

Instead, the leverage necessary to safeguard U.S. interests in the Gulf should be sought out *incrementally*, by maintaining a careful balance of relations among all the power centers in the area, including Iraq and Saudi Arabia. Again, Washington will find it worthwhile to pursue a long-term relationship with Iraq.

"Important changes are taking place in Iraq. . . . The potential for these changes to exert a positive influence on long-term U.S. interests in the Middle East and the Gulf should not be ignored."

But as with any Arab state, the real litmus test of whether Iraqi-U.S. relations have a viable future depends on Baghdad's attitude toward Israel and the Arab-Israeli conflict. In this respect, there are suprising developments to take note of: The Iraqi regime, in 1978 and 1982, took the unprecedented, but little-noticed, step of signing on with Arab League declarations—the summit communiqués from Baghdad and Fez—that accepted the principle of a negotiated settlement with Israel. A development that attracted wider attention was the publication of

Hussein's 1982 interview with U.S. Rep. Stephen Solarz, in which the Iraqi leader was quoted as saying that "the existence of a secure state for the Israelis" was necessary to regional peace.

Iraq's Moderation

From the standpoint of U.S. policy, Iraq's moderation on such issues took on concrete significance when, early in 1982, then Secretary of State Alexander Haig removed Iraq from the list of countries supporting international terrorism. The State Department has since successfully defused several congressional attempts to put Iraq back on the terrorism list and at one point affirmed that Iraq had cooperated repeatedly and actively with the United States "against specific terrorist threats to shared interests." Iraq also gave a mild endorsement to the U.S.-backed May 17, 1983, agreement on foreign troop withdrawals from Lebanon. It also gave indirect backing to the Reagan peace initiative of September 1982 by fending off Syrian pressures against Jordan, thereby giving King Hussein wider latitude to pursue the Reagan proposals.

Iraq's public pronouncements on the Arab-Israeli conflict now routinely indicate that it will accept any settlement that the Palestinians accept, while also asserting that Iraq is not a frontline state and therefore not a direct party to the conflict. This represents a dramatic softening in Iraqi attitudes from only a few years ago. Equally important to note is that Israel and its supporters in the United States have begun to take note. In March 1987, a current vice president of the American Jewish Committee, Alfred Moses, suggested that Israel might be mistaken in continuing to regard Iraq as "intractable" on the issue of Arab-Israeli peace and argued that the possibility of an Iraqi move toward peace "is too great for Jerusalem to ignore." Several months later, an editorial in the *Jerusalem Post* struck the same chord, declaring that "Iraq's enmity [to Israel] can no longer be taken for granted as no lesser than Syria's and as far worse than Iran's. The time has come for a reassessment of Israeli policy."

This same message—it is time for a policy reassessment—should also be directed to those who have instinctively opposed the ephemeral (and thus far relatively ineffectual) U.S. tilt toward Iraq in the Gulf war. There is a serious possibility that important changes are taking place in Iraq's domestic situation and foreign policies. The potential for these changes to exert a positive influence on long-term U.S. interests in the Middle East and the Gulf should not be ignored.

Frederick W. Axelgard is a fellow in Middle East studies at Georgetown University and the author of Iraq: The Gulf War and the Struggle for Legitimacy.

"What has not been made clear by the administration in its 'neutral' posturing is that ... Iraq is a Marxist client state of the Soviet Union."

The US Should Not Support Iraq

Jane Ingraham

The curious case of the country that attacked a U.S. ship, killed 37 American crewmen, and emerged with "much improved relations" must be unique in history. According to an analysis of diplomatic relations between Iraq and the United States, ties actually are stronger and more friendly since the attack on the *USS Stark*. The reason for this, says the suave and impeccably dressed Nizar Hamdoon, Iraq's ambassador to the U.S., is that Iraq's President Saddam Hussein sent an unprecedented apology for the "incident" to President Reagan and promised compensation; this was accepted by the United States and now relations are "better than ever."

Not that the United States did not look into the matter. It sent a team of experts led by Rear Admiral David Rogers, a member of the Council on Foreign Relations (CFR), to Iraq to confer with officials there. Although "unable" to interview the pilot who fired on the *Stark*, these experts concluded that the attack was unintentional, caused by pilot error. Two *Stark* officers were reprimanded for "unpreparedness," and their naval careers were terminated.

Aligned with Our Attacker

These strange events come at a time when the devastating war between Iraq and Iran is an old story; hostilities have been depopulating both countries at the rate of about 100,000 per year for over six years. Hundreds of tankers flying the flags of 30 nations have already been struck in the Persian Gulf. Nothing has changed in this situation except the attack on the *Stark*. But that was enough. Suddenly Mr. Reagan sees it as a national priority to dispatch our warships to the Middle East for the purpose of escorting Kuwaiti tankers placed under the protection of the American flag. And, *mirabile*

dictu, because Kuwait is on Iraq's side in the Iran-Iraq war, we have in effect positioned ourselves on the side of our apologetic attacker, tipping the scales heavily against its enemy, Iran. This must be gratifying to the parents and wives of the deceased naval personnel. Congress has joined in by tacking an amendment on the trade bill, which calls for an international trade embargo against Iran if that country harms our interests in the Gulf, while other officials call for a military posture just short of war.

What has not been made clear by the administration in its "neutral" posturing is that Kuwait is Iraq's lifeline, and Iraq is a Marxist client state of the Soviet Union. Little noticed until recently, Kuwait is a tiny, fabulously rich sheikdom bordering Iraq at the north end of the Persian Gulf, ruled for more than 200 years by the al-Sabah family. The present emir has cordial relations with Moscow. He was the first of the Gulf state rulers to establish diplomatic relations with the Soviet Union, having done so in 1963. . . . More importantly, he allows Kuwait's Shuaiba Harbor to be used for unloading Soviet arms, which are then transported in long military convoys through Kuwait to Iraq. Billions of dollars of Kuwaiti oil revenue support Iraq's war effort. Iraqi planes are allowed to use Kuwaiti air space, but the United States is not allowed to land its helicopters on Kuwaiti soil; even so, the United States is allowed to put U.S. flags on Kuwaiti ships and to provide military protection.

Iraq's Hostilities

Assistance from Kuwait and the Soviet Union has enabled Iraq to continue fighting. Once a great oil power and fabulously wealthy, Iraq gained a reputation as one of the world's most lavish spenders on military equipment. Now, its resources exhausted by the war—which it started—it is virtually bankrupt. But its Arab friends, fearful of the spread of militant Islamic fundamentalism by

"What Are We Doing in the Persian Gulf?" by Jane Ingraham first appeared in the August 31, 1987 issue of *The New American* magazine and is reprinted by permission of the publisher. All rights reserved.

Iran's Shi'ite Moslems, will never allow Iraq to be defeated because of lack of funds. At the moment, Iraq is winning the tanker war at sea; Iran is winning the land war. Iran's most telling military success thus far has been the closing of the port of Basra, Iraq's only outlet to the Gulf, forcing Iraq to use the long route through Kuwait.

But Iraq is currently initiating most of the hostilities, being responsible for over 60 percent of all tanker attacks, according to the State Department. Iran, which ships most of its million-barrel daily output through the Gulf in tankers, is particularly vulnerable at sea. Thus Iraq, which sends virtually all its oil overland or through pipelines, stands to gain by continuing the tanker war. In fact, Iran started attacking Gulf shipping only after the Iraqi lead. In June [1987], Iran's Prime Minister Mir Hossein Mussavi said that his country would stop tanker attacks if Iraq also refrained. Iraq has ignored this initiative.

"It now becomes clear that we have sent our men to risk their lives in the Persian Gulf for the benefit of two countries with close ties to Moscow."

Iraq's soft spot, however, is Kuwaiti ships carrying the oil that finances the Iraqi war effort. Mr. Reagan has obligingly stepped in to protect this Achilles heel.

It now becomes clear that we have sent our men to risk their lives in the Persian Gulf for the benefit of two countries with close ties to Moscow. This, of course, is not the way Mr. Reagan has presented it. He has given several explanations.

Right of Free Navigation?

One is that we must uphold the principle of freedom of navigation. The right of unimpeded access to and free passage on the seas, he says, is basic to international commerce and must be defended. No one disputes this principle. But whose right of free passage are we defending? Everyone's, or just Kuwait's? Since we apparently will retaliate only if U.S.-flagged Kuwaiti ships or our own naval escorts are harmed, Iraq has the green light to continue destroying Iranian shipping. In addition, it gives Iran the same signal for its attacks on tankers operating under other countries' flags. Such an instance occurred when Iran struck an American-operated tanker operating under the Liberian flag, and Mr. Reagan said he saw no need to respond.

Yet Mr. Reagan offers as another explanation the fact that we must protect the free flow of oil, which is vital to our own interests and to those of Europe and Japan. The more Mr. Reagan explains, the

deeper appear the inconsistencies. As S. Fred Singer, visiting eminent scholar at George Mason University put it in the *Wall Street Journal* for June 9, 1987:

> To prevent a world oil supply interruption—if this is indeed America's purpose—the U.S. must not only stop tanker attacks by Iran, but also Iraqi attacks on Iranian oil carried by Iran or by third parties. Otherwise U.S. actions would be construed as a direct military involvement in the Iran-Iraq conflict, rather than as an undertaking to protect oil shipments to Free World consumers or to uphold the principle of free navigation.

Exactly. In addition, it seems only too obvious that the concept of shielding tankers from air attack, land-based missiles, speedboats, and mines is bound to prove inadequate. Oil moves not only in tankers, but through pipelines, oil-field installations, loading platforms, and other links in the transport chain. Iran can disrupt the flow of oil by attacking any of the links in the transport chain; the passage of tankers through the Persian Gulf is only one of those links.

If we are not protecting either the free flow of oil or the right of free navigation for everyone, *why are we in the Persian Gulf?*

Oil Market Stability?

Let us pause here and look at the question of oil supply and price. Although latest estimates are that we receive only six percent of our oil from the Gulf, fear of a cutoff has caused oil refiners to rush to build up crude oil inventories just in case, sending the price at the end of July [1987] to $21 per barrel from $18 one month earlier. Psychological reaction left over from previous oil disturbances could rapidly push the price at least 20 percent higher. But world demand is flattening and there is presently an oversupply, two factors that cause industry analysts to say high prices would be short-lived. The Organization of Petroleum Exporting Countries (OPEC) is already obliging with sharply expanded output. As oil producers step up production to capitalize on the price escalation, they are planting the seeds of another oil glut and a repeat of last year's price collapse. Philip Verleger, visiting fellow at the Institute for International Economics, stated that, "unless the oil-exporting countries really put the brake on production, we'd see the 1986 oil price collapse all over again—only faster, within three months."

How about supplies to the rest of the Free World? The truth is that, while still of first importance, the Persian Gulf is shrinking as an oil shipping route. Current volume is about 8.4 million barrels per day, or a little more than one-third of the world's total oil trade. This is down sharply from 14 million barrels per day in the early 1980s, which was 48 percent of world oil trade. In case of a blockage of the Strait of Hormuz, about five million barrels per day of the lost volume could be made up for by diversion through existing pipelines and increased production outside the Gulf. The Paris-based International Energy Agency [IEA] is not worried. The *Wall Street Journal* reported on July 23rd [1987]:

> An IEA spokesman cited available Middle East pipeline capacity as well as two to three million barrels a day total spare producing capacity in Venezuela, Mexico, Indonesia and Nigeria. Government stockpiles among the 21 economically advanced nations total 103 million tons, versus 25 million in 1979. Commercial inventories are also edging up rapidly. Indeed, prices could fall because of the increase in inventories. . . .

If there is no real danger of a drop in oil supply or a sustained price increase, *why are we in the Persian Gulf?*

Challenge to the Soviets?

Another explanation Mr. Reagan has given is that of containing the Soviets: We must prevent an expanded Soviet role in the Gulf and arrest Soviet influence there. Addressing this point in June [1987], Mr. Reagan said:

> If we don't do the job, the Soviets will. If we fail to protect the tankers, we would abdicate our role as a naval power. And we would open opportunities for the Soviets to move into this chokepoint of the free world's oil flow.

[Former] Defense Secretary Caspar Weinberger, a member of the CFR, supported Mr. Reagan and strongly backed our intervention as a way to head off the Soviets. Under Secretary of State Michael Armacost, also a member of the CFR, defended the increased U.S. presence by arguing that oil supplies might be jeopardized if the Soviet Union becomes the chief protector in the area. Going along with the decision to intervene were Marine Corps General P.X. Kelley, now retired but a member of the Joint Chiefs of Staff when the decision was made, and Admiral Carlisle Trost, the Chief of Naval Operations. Both General Kelley and Admiral Trost are members of the CFR.

In view of the facts presented thus far, this anti-Soviet posture by our top officials is shocking in its transparency. Not only are we protecting *only* Kuwaiti tankers, disregarding the rest of the "free world's oil flow," but of the two countries we are helping, one (Iraq) has long aligned itself with the Soviet Union, and the other (Kuwait) has taken the lead in bringing the Soviets into the region. Most importantly, our aid did not prevent Kuwait from also inviting the Soviet Union to escort its tankers (some of which are leased from the Soviets), thus giving Moscow something it has long sought, a locally sanctioned military presence in the Gulf. Instead of keeping the Soviets from "doing the job," what we are more likely to see, according to White House Chief of Staff Howard Baker (CFR), is the United States and the USSR acting together as "co-guarantors of peace" in the Gulf. As partners, we would work together to see to it that Marxist Iraq's war effort is sustained.

Furthermore, in view of recent history Mr. Reagan's concern about protecting the Strait of Hormuz chokepoint rings hollow indeed. Since we have already witnessed how the critical maritime chokepoints of the Suez and Panama Canals were maneuvered out of Free World control by Presidents Eisenhower and Carter, it would hardly be surprising if Hormuz ends up being added to the list. Mr. Reagan also knows that not only the Strait of Hormuz, but also the route around South Africa connecting the Indian and Atlantic Oceans, is vital to the movement of Persian Gulf oil to the West. Yet, thanks to his failure to support freedom fighters, the Soviets are positioned in Mozambique on the Indian Ocean and Angola on the Atlantic; if Mr. Reagan continues destabilizing the government of South Africa, the Cape of Good Hope will also fall into Marxist hands and consolidate Soviet control of the 4,000 mile route.

At any rate, if our tanker shield is enhancing rather than diminishing Soviet interests in the Persian Gulf, *why are we there?*

US Credibility?

An additional and especially curious explanation for Mr. Reagan's initiative has been expressed by top officials as "a need to rebuild American credibility in the Gulf after the arms-to-Iran fiasco." National Security Advisor Frank Carlucci (CFR) advocated the escort plan as a way to "restore American credibility" in the region. Under Secretary of State Michael Armacost (CFR) said that a reason for our stepped-up presence is "the administration's loss-of-face following the Iranian arms-for-hostages deals." Under questioning, Mr. Armacost agreed that the need to show "moderate" Arab states that the United States could be a "reliable friend" was "heightened" by the arms shipments to Iran.

"Of the two countries we are helping, one (Iraq) has long aligned itself with the Soviet Union."

What are we to make of this? Why are we being told that help to one despotic state is an indication of "integrity" and "reliability," but help to another constitutes "loss-of-face"? One thing is clear; the signal we are sending to Iran comes close to being a declaration of war. Our top officials are unanimously agreed that we are prepared to attack; a preemptive strike has even been mentioned. White House Chief of Staff Howard Baker (CFR) said that "we ought to have the military might . . . to do whatever we need to do . . . and the Iranians ought to wonder about that." National Security Advisor Frank Carlucci (CFR) said: "They should know . . . that our ships are prepared." Nicholas Veliotes (CFR), Assistant Secretary of State for the Middle East in the first years of the Reagan Administration, explained that "you must retaliate or you have no credibility, even though by retaliating you are drawn further in. . . ." Admiral William J. Crowe (CFR), chairman of the Joint Chiefs of Staff, has asserted that U.S. policy should include automatic retaliation for any harm to our interests by Iran. Both Mr. Reagan and Defense Secretary Weinberger (CFR) have suggested that the United States might launch a preemptive strike against Iranian antiship missiles if they are emplaced.

Conjuring Up an Enemy

Never has an enemy been so dramatically conjured up in so short a time! Less than a year ago we were selling arms to the Ayatollah; what has happened to change the scene so radically? Incredibly, we are being told that the turning point against Iran came with the attack on the *USS Stark* by *Iraq*. One example of this line of thinking appeared in a *Wall Street Journal* article dated June 29, 1987:

> Iran's posture stiffened, in the view of American analysts, when an Iraqi missile struck the U.S.S. Stark in the Gulf this spring. The Stark incident focused attention on the Gulf and on the U.S. agreement to escort Kuwaiti tankers. That attention made it impossible for Tehran to ignore what it saw as a challenge in its own backyard, U.S. officials believe. So Iran has grown more belligerent . . . and this threat must be met.

Leaving aside the question of *who* has grown more belligerent, this ridiculous nonsense is being passed off as a *casus belli*. But at least we now see many of the effects of the *Stark* being struck. Like a mini Pearl Harbor, the only confirmed facts about the incident are 37 deaths and the ruining of two careers. Captain G. R. Brindel, the *Stark*'s skipper, emphasized in his statement that the attack was totally *unexpected*; there was no reason to believe the Iraqi plane was hostile. Yet apparently, the *Stark* did issue two warnings to the Iraqi Mirage. But Representative Les Aspin (CFR), chairman of the House Armed Services Committee, closed his investigation by holding the skipper responsible, saying "it isn't certain" when the warnings were issued, and furthermore, "Iraqi pilots often ignore their international radios and thus don't respond to such warnings." So Captain Brindel was demoted, discharged in dishonor, and someone's idea of justice achieved. When Iraqi Ambassador Nizar Hamdoon was asked if the pilot had been punished, he replied that, since the attack was unintentional, nothing specific had happened to him.

Then there is the "inevitable" opposition to Mr. Reagan's plan in the Democratic-controlled Senate. As it began to mount and become a problem,

Senator Claiborne Pell (CFR) sponsored a resolution that would have forced the United States to renege on its commitment to reflag. The day before it was to be considered, however, Senator Pell, claiming that reneging would "further the administration's retreat from influence in the Middle East," withdrew his resolution and the opposition fizzled.

The Heart of the Matter

We come now to the heart of the matter—Iran. The Soviet bid for control of Iran has been in progress for many years. What we are now seeing is the culmination of a strategy whereby Washington and Moscow have been acting in tandem to achieve that objective. Begun in 1977 under the Carter Administration, this strategy has put an intense anti-American religious fanatic in place in Iran and has created a situation that the Soviets can use to their advantage. Yet only seven years ago, under the Shah, Iran was a major ally of the United States and, with Israel, the most pro-Western country in the Middle East.

"All we can know for sure is that this foreign policy scenario . . . will end in disaster for the Free World."

It is important to repeat, however briefly, how this disastrous turnabout occurred, for Iran is among the planet's most vital territories. Its importance to the Free World cannot be overemphasized. Its geographic location on the southern border of the USSR, its warm-water ports the Czars dreamed of, and its oil fields, which produce 80 percent of Europe's and Japan's petroleum, should have made one of our highest priorities the befriending and protection of Iran. For many years, this was the case, until Mr. Carter took office and joined the Soviet Union in a pincer movement to destroy the Shah.

While Carter depicted the Shah as a "gross violator of human rights" and forced major "liberal" concessions that aided internal subversion, a flood of Soviet-trained agents infiltrated the country and made common cause with the powerful Shi'ite clergy, who, ironically, were disaffected from the Shah because he had sought to institute modern day human rights. Ayatollah (meaning "reflection of God") Ruhollah Khomeini assumed leadership of these Islamic-Marxists and, as the situation deteriorated through massive street demonstrations and riots (believed to have been organized by the CIA), he was formally endorsed by the Communist Tudeh Party.

As the Ayatollah's Shi'ite revolution merged with the Communists, Mr. Carter began demanding that the Shah abdicate and leave Iran. By the time

General Robert Huyser and George Ball (CFR) went to Tehran to force the Shah out, the outcome was clear. Huyser directly threatened the military with a break in diplomatic relations and a cutoff of arms if it moved to support its monarch. Later these top generals were all executed by the Khomeini regime.

A Crisis at Hand

Since 1979, the question has been how long the aged and ill Khomeini will be allowed to remain as the front man before Moscow moves to replace him and consolidate its power with a more pro-Soviet puppet. Perhaps we are about to see the answer to that question. Obviously a crisis is at hand, or Mr. Reagan would not have made this precipitous move and struggled to disguise it with a tissue of sophistries.

Although our ostensible role in the Gulf is to help Iraq and make a show of force against Iran, we cannot know, until after the fact, what tactics the Insiders plan to use to attain their final objective. Although direct military intervention is not their usual way of doing things (Afghanistan being a notable exception), we do know that the Soviets have five divisions on Iran's northern border. Perhaps there is intelligence that the Ayatollah is on his deathbed. All we can know for sure is that this foreign policy scenario, like all the others, is being masterminded by members of the Council on Foreign Relations and, like all the others, will end in disaster for the Free World.

The fall of Iran to the Ayatollah was a major catastrophe for the West; the fall of Iran to the Soviets would be the beginning of the end.

Jane Ingraham is a contributing editor to The New American, *a conservative biweekly magazine.*

"Laws have been broken, the Constitution disregarded, Congress has been snubbed, and the American people ignored."

The Iran-Contra Affair Was Illegal

Michael Ratner

The reason for the lack of fire in the [Iran-contra] hearings and the debates is not difficult to discern. The constitutional issues and abuse of power by the President are important to Congress, but not as important as the continuation of U.S. economic and political hegemony in the world. The President's policies, in his view, were necessary to insure such domination. Congress will apparently do little or nothing that threatens a hegemony in which it also believes.

But if the Congress has not been overly concerned, the American public should be. What is at issue is not only a crisis involving members of government lying to Congress, falsifying records and chronologies, misleading the Attorney General and other cabinet members, destroying key documents, and misusing tax exemptions, but a constitutional crisis of the most serious sort. In defense of his actions, the President has challenged the most fundamental precepts of the Constitution. He has claimed the right to disregard laws passed by Congress, fight wars contrary to Congressional prohibitions, and involve himself with privateers. Separation of powers and the system of checks and balances, the bedrock of the U.S. constitutional system, have been considered by the President to be mere formalities waived in the interests of what he deems to be "national security." Congress and the media seek to avoid dealing with this issue.

The President has offered three defenses to the revelations concerning arming and directing the contras. First, he claimed he did not know and did not approve of the operation. Second, he said that even if he knew, it was not a violation of law and not a violation of the Boland Amendment. Third, and most serious, he asserted that his authority over foreign affairs included the war power and that Congress could not limit him whether through the Boland Amendment or otherwise.

His first defense—that he did not know of the efforts to arm the contras—is untenable in light of the evidence revealed at the hearings. In fact, he has been exposed as lying about his role in and knowledge of the raising of private and foreign monies for the contras at a time when such activities were prohibited by Congress. The Tower Commission painted a picture of a President disengaged and remote, who was not aware of the manner in which his subordinates carried out the funding of the contras. The President himself, at the commencement of the hearings, said, "I have no detailed information."

A Cover-Up

The hearings revealed a very different President, one who encouraged aid to the contras and who knew of the arms resupply operation. Former National [Security] Adviser Robert McFarlane testified to briefing the President "dozens of times" about what he and his subordinates were doing to fund the contras, and Admiral [John] Poindexter testified that he had informed the President of the NSC [National Security Council] operation to fund the contras. The President spoke with Saudi Arabia's King Fahd about Saudi multi-million dollar contributions to the contras. Shortly after this meeting, the Saudis doubled their contribution to the contras to $2 million per month. Frequently, the President was asked to meet with major fundraisers or give talks to potential donors.

To deflect attention from his role described above, the President claimed that the only issue of concern at the hearings was whether or not he had knowledge of the diversion of funds from the Iran arms sales to the contras. He asserted a lack of knowledge regarding the diversion. As is obvious

Michael Ratner, "Contragate, Covert Action and the Constitution," *Social Policy*, Summer 1987. Copyright 1987 by Social Policy Corporation.

from the foregoing discussion, this is not the only question. But even on this issue, there is evidence showing he may have had knowledge of the diversion that elaborate measures were taken to cover-up.

On November 22, 1986, Justice Department investigators found in Oliver North's files a five-page memo from North detailing the steps necessary to divert $12 million from Iran arms sales to the contras. The document, designed for Presidential approval or disapproval, was seen by national security adviser Poindexter. When found, the document did not have attached to it the cover letter indicating that it went to the President, but North, when questioned, asked whether it had been found with a cover letter. The document was found the day after North had shredded hundreds of documents. It may be too late to ever prove conclusively that the document went to the President, and Admiral Poindexter denied that it did.

The President can no longer defend himself very well on the facts. He was the author of the policy to aid the contras, encouraged and planned it, and was a key participant.

The President also relied on a second defense. Although he and the NSC raised funds and otherwise assisted the contras during a period when the Boland Amendment's prohibitions were in effect, he argued that the law had no applicability to him and the NSC. This is an argument cut from whole cloth. If he is wrong, and he is, impeachment should follow as a matter of course.

The Boland Amendment provided that no monies available to the "CIA [Central Intelligence Agency], the Department of Defense, or any other agency or entity of the United States involved in intelligence activities" could be used to support, directly or indirectly, the contras. The Amendment was in effect for two fiscal years—from October 1984 through September 1986. For the latter half of this period, from approximately August 1985 on, the Boland Amendment contained the additional prohibition on soliciting funds from other countries for the contras, at least to the extent such solicitation was based upon an express or implied understanding that the donor country would receive U.S. military assistance.

Violated Boland Amendment

It was during this two-year period when North, the CIA, and others were carrying out the supply operation and when [fundraiser] Carl Channell, with the President's help, was soliciting money for the operations. Likewise, the President's approach to the Saudis took place when such activities were illegal.

The President's chief argument to escape from under the prohibitions of the Boland Amendment is that neither the NSC nor the President are agencies or entities involved in intelligence activities and, thus, that amendment has no application to them.

The President claims he is supported in this argument by an opinion issued by an attorney with the Intelligence Oversight Board. The attorney who drafted the opinion admitted that he had spent only five minutes asking North about his activities and that North was a friend of his. The attorney was a novice who had flunked the bar exam four times.

"Obviously, Congress meant to cover the NSC in the Boland Amendment prohibitions."

The Administration took an entirely different position on the meaning of the Boland Amendment before Congress in 1985. At that time, both National Security Adviser McFarlane and Assistant Secretary [of State] Langhorne C. Motley assured Congress that the NSC and the entire Administration were obeying the Boland Amendment's prohibitions and that there was no assistance to the contras, direct or indirect. As Motley stated:

> Nobody is trying to play games with member[s] of Congress. That resolution stands, and it will continue to stand; and it says no direct or indirect. And that is pretty plain English; it does not have to be written by any bright young lawyers. And we are going to comply with that.

Congress was also assured that monies were not being solicited from other countries. Undersecretary of State Elliott Abrams knowingly lied about this to Congress.

There is also no foundation for the President's claim that the NSC is not an intelligence agency or entity. The statutory definition of an intelligence agency is "any department, agency, or other entity of the United States involved in intelligence-related activities." The functions of the NSC are set forth in an Executive Order signed by President Reagan in 1981:

> The NSC shall act as the highest Executive Branch entity that provides review of, guidance for, and direction to the conduct of all national foreign intelligence, counterintelligence, and special activities, and attendant policies and programs.

In addition, the NSC reviews all covert operations and submits recommendations to the President for approval.

An Absurd Argument

In view of the NSC's role in directing all intelligence gathering, it is absurd to argue that it is not involved in "intelligence-related activities." Obviously, Congress meant to cover the NSC in the Boland Amendment prohibitions. Any activities undertaken for it or its employees to support the contras were completely unauthorized.

The only remaining question is whether the

President was covered by the prohibitions. To the extent he cooperated with, assisted, approved, or directed the NSC in its contra-related activities he is a co-conspirator and is covered. It is known that he engaged in some or all of these activities. It is also known that he solicited funds from the Saudis and that this prohibition attached to all government officials.

The patent absurdity of the President's argument that he and the NSC were not covered can be seen in the following example. Congress desired to end all support to the contras. It outlawed aid from those agencies authorized to engage in covert operations of the type that were involved in Nicaragua. It did not need to outlaw aid from entities that were not permitted to assist covert operation. So it follows that there was no need for the law to cover the Department of Health and Human Services [HHS] or every other agency of the U.S. government. The President was never authorized on his own to aid or assist covert operations. There was no need for Congress to cover him. If the President's argument is accepted, it would mean that HHS or any other federal entity not explicitly named by Congress could aid the contras.

The President, recognizing the frivolousness of his factual and legal position, relied in the end on what he calls his inherent power over foreign affairs that he asserts Congress cannot limit. This, according to him, includes the power to assist the contras or, in other words, to engage in war: the Boland Amendment cannot limit his powers. This last defense is most dangerous. It is an assertion that the President is above the law and is contrary to the text of the Constitution and the clear intention of the framers. At a time when Attorney General Meese is telling us that the Constitution should have the meaning it was intended to have 200 years ago, this Presidential claim is especially spurious.

War Powers

The Constitution could not be clearer on who has the war powers. Congress is given the power to declare war, grant letters of marque and reprisal, raise, support and regulate the armed forces, and organize the militia. On the other hand, the President is named Commander-in-Chief and given the power to commission officers. He has the authority to conduct wars authorized or declared by Congress, but no power to start or continue them without Congressional approval.

The drafting of the war powers clauses of the Constitution confirm the limited nature of the President's role. The framers considered the war power to be extremely dangerous, and particularly as a young and weak nation the United States had a strong interest in maintaining peace and neutrality. The framers felt that Congress would be less likely to get the nation into war than a President who

might do so for self-aggrandizement. Requiring both houses of Congress to agree would make going to war difficult; as George Mason, one of the framers, stated, he was "for clogging rather than facilitating war, [but] for facilitating peace." The only exception to the requirement that the Congress initiate war is the President's authority to repel sudden attacks—an obvious need when Congress would have no time to meet.

"The President as a creature of the Constitution has only the powers granted him by that document."

Presidents have on more than the present occasion attempted to initiate or continue wars without Congressional authority. Normally an excuse was given such as the need to protect U.S. lives and property. Assertions analogous to Reagan's—that the President alone has the authority to make war against another country—are few. President Truman made such a claim in Korea; Presidents Johnson and Nixon did so with regard to Vietnam. In one important respect, President Reagan's assertion of inherent authority to make war is novel. No President ever claimed that he, independent of Congress and contrary to its will, could raise the money to arm an army and fight wars completely on his own. It was hoped by many in Congress that such exercises of power were ended by passage of the War Powers Resolution, the reporting requirements of the Foreign Assistance Act, and the Hughes-Ryan Amendment, which gave Congress some authority over the CIA. Because the President is asserting such authority despite this recent legislation and the Constitution, his claims represent a serious undermining of the Constitution as well as a grave danger.

Undermining Separation of Powers

Under the normal functioning of the Constitution the Congress need not pass a law restricting Presidential or CIA spending for a war. The Boland Amendment should not have been necessary. To engage in war, as has been said, some form of Congressional assent is necessary. The President as a creature of the Constitution has only the powers granted him by that document. His powers are particularly narrow in areas where authority is given to another branch.

To the extent the President can make any argument that there is a loophole for small wars or war when U.S. soldiers are not doing the fighting (and incidently this argument is completely without foundation) the Boland Amendment removes even that spurious claim. It expresses a clear Congressional intent to stop the support and funding of the contras. It specifies very clearly what is and is not allowed. It is one thing for the President to assert some authority when Congress has remained silent; it is quite another in the face of Congressional disapproval. That is a most serious violation of the fundamental tenets of the Constitution and a serious undermining of the separation of powers.

"[The Reagan] Administration should not be permitted to make decisions that have a permanent and adverse effect on our lives and those of others throughout the world."

President Truman made an analogous argument when he seized and operated the steel mills of the nation in order to avoid a strike that he believed would cripple the U.S. war effort in Korea. Like President Reagan, Truman asserted that he had the inherent authority to seize the steel mills to protect the national security and prosecute the war, claiming he did not need Congressional authority to do so. The Supreme Court declared the seizure unconstitutional. Justice [Robert H.] Jackson pointed out that whatever the President's powers were when Congress approved of his actions, Presidential authority to seize the mills when Congress disapproved was at its lowest ebb. To sustain seizure of the mills—or, by analogy, contra funding—the President would need to demonstrate that the Constitution gave him alone the particular power and that the Congress was precluded from acting. This is obviously not so with regard to the war powers.

Impeachment

There are ample grounds for impeachment of the President and other high executive officials. Although less than two years is left in [President Reagan's] term, impeachment is not academic. This Administration should not be permitted to make decisions that have a permanent and adverse effect on our lives and those of others throughout the world. Impeachment proceedings would stop appointments to the Supreme Court; they might slow the war against Nicaragua and other covert operations now in the planning stage. They would expose the secret government that has taken over the White House. In the longer term, impeachment would demonstrate that limitations on the President contained in laws and in the Constitution have meaning and cannot be violated with impunity. Impeachment hearings might also give us an opportunity to expose the deeper crimes of this and other administrations—the making of aggressive war

against countries struggling for self-determination.

Article II, Section 4 of the Constitution provides that "the President, Vice President, and all civil officers of the United States shall be removed from Office on Impeachment for, or Conviction of Treason, Bribery or other high Crimes and Misdemeanors." An impeachable offense need not be a crime or an indictable offense. As [Thomas] Cooley, in his *Principles of Constitutional Law,* stated:

> They [high crimes and misdemeanors] are not necessarily offenses against the general laws. . . . It is often found that offenses of a very serious nature by high officers are not offenses against the criminal code, but consist in abuses or betrayals of trust, or inexcusable neglects of duty.

Thus, if the President or other high executive officials used their authority to violate the Constitution or other law of the land, impeachment is appropriate. [John] Pomeroy, in his treatise *Constitutional Law,* writes that a President who has "knowingly and intentionally violated the express terms of the Constitution, or of a statute which charged him with an official duty" is impeachable.

There are numerous grounds upon which the House of Representatives can draw up articles of impeachment. Representative [Henry] Gonzalez has taken an important first step and introduced a resolution of impeachment. It lists numerous violations of law in connection with the President's failure to follow various statutes regarding the shipment of Hawk and TOW missiles to Iran and cites the President's knowledge of or failure to prevent the diversion of funds to Nicaragua. However, both future public discussion and bills of impeachment should include more serious charges.

The President takes an oath to "preserve, protect, and defend the Constitution." This includes the constitutional obligation "to take care that the Laws be faithfully executed." The President cannot decide for himself which laws to obey. So, for example, his claim that the Boland Amendment unconstitutionally restricts his powers and that he need not have obeyed it is not a decision he was authorized to make; that decision is left to the courts. The President must obey the law until the courts permit him to do otherwise.

Overriding the Constitution

The claim that the President has the inherent power to continue the war against Nicaragua is an assertion that he has powers superior to and that override the Constitution. Such an assertion of executive authority must not be permitted to stand. Impeachment is necessary if we are to have a President with limited powers who remains a creature of the Constitution. Assertions of inherent authority in the name of national security lead to imposition of martial law at home and war abroad. It is but a short step to the justifications used by the

Argentinian generals to round up and cause to disappear thousands of Argentinian citizens. Recent revelations concerning a plan for martial law to combat civil unrest demonstrate that these fears are not fanciful.

While the President and others have committed serious violations of the Constitution, the most egregious crime they have committed is the international crime of initiating a war of aggression, which constitutes a crime against peace—a fundamental offense against the laws of civilization. The Nuremberg Judgment emphasized the serious nature of a crime against peace:

> To initate a war of aggression, therefore, is not only an international crime; it is the supreme international crime differing only from other war crimes in that it contains within itself the accumulated evil of the whole.

Some people may question whether a crime against peace is an impeachable offense. Professor Richard Falk answered this a number of years ago in discussing Nixon's impeachment. He pointed out that impeachment should include the war of aggression Nixon carried out against Vietnam, Laos, and Cambodia.

> But surely the Constitution is flexible enough to embrace a range of activities that endangers national, even human survival and has long been reduced to legal form.

There can be no real dispute regarding the President's initiation of a war of aggression against Nicaragua. The World Court, in its June 1986 decision, ruled that by training, arming, equipping, funding, and supplying the contras, the United States violated its obligations under customary international law not to use force against another state: in other words, a war crime, a crime against peace. The World Court ordered the United States immediately to refrain and desist from all acts of war against Nicaragua.

Unfortunately, neither the President nor the Congress has done so. The Congress, by voting $100 million in aid, is in violation of international law and the World Court judgment. For this reason it is extremely unlikely that Congress will ever consider impeachment on the real reason for the present crisis—the illegal war against Nicaragua.

The Hearings Failed

We must ask why the hearings were such a bloodless affair. The hard questions were not asked. The serious constitutional issues were not addressed. Members of the select committees, particularly the Democrats, went out of their way to stress the bipartisan, neutral, and nonprosecutorial nature of the hearings. The Congress is not blind. It is aware of the serious violations of law and violations of the Constitution committed by the President. It knows that the President is asserting unprecedented

authority. Yet we heard not a word about impeachment from the select committees.

The primary answer to the question is political and not legal. Although many of us would like to believe there are serious divisions in Congress regarding our Nicaragua policy, this is not so. While there are divisions about supporting the contras, at least at the present time, there is near unanimity about the nature of the Nicaraguan government and the importance of U.S. interests of changing that government. It was a Democrat-controlled House that approved military assistance to the contras. The only debate in Congress concerns the method for making the Sandinistas cry "uncle." Should the United States employ only economic and diplomatic pressure, or military means as well?

"The Congress is not blind. It is aware of the serious violations of law and violations of the Constitution committed by the President."

The members of the select committees and other members of Congress have bent over backward to detail their abhorrence of the Sandinistas and the Nicaraguan government. The majority of the select committees voted in favor of contra aid. Legislation passed by Congress concerning Nicaragua reflects this consensus.

Frequently, it has passed legislation outlining the alleged horrors of the Sandinistas. So, for example, even the legislation cutting off military aid to the contras for fiscal year 1986, the Boland Amendment, outlined the following supposed Sandinista horrors: Ortega's 1985 trip to the Soviet Union; Nicaragua's close military ties to Cuba, the Soviet Union and its Warsaw Pact allies; the alleged failure to reduce Cuban military advisers in Nicaragua; the continuing military buildup considered threatening to Nicaragua's neighbors; the curtailment of individual liberties, political expression, freedom of worship, and the independence of the media; the subordination of the military, judicial, and internal security functions to the party; and the efforts of the Sandinistas to spread its influence and ideology.

The consensus about Nicaragua has not changed despite the revelations at the hearings. In May 1987, the Democrat-controlled House defeated legislation prohibiting military maneuvers in Honduras and Costa Rica and rejected an amendment prohibiting the building of military roads and airports in Honduras—roads and airports that are used to support the contras. In June 1987, the House passed the Walker-Smith Amendment limiting travel to Nicaragua by U.S. persons if the purpose of the travel is to assist or aid the military operations of the government of Nicaragua. In opposing this Amendment, liberals who are against aid to the contras found it necessary to condemn the Sandinistas.

As long as there is a consensus regarding the nature of the Nicaraguan government, it will be difficult to seriously modify U.S. policy. With a consensus about Nicaragua, the actions of the President, the NSC, and the CIA are viewed as an attempt to achieve goals shared by Congress and many Americans. While the law and the Constitution may have been violated, they were violated for a good cause. Against such a backdrop, it is no wonder that talk of impeachment has been nonexistent.

"President Reagan has truly established a government of the Executive, by the Executive, and for the Executive."

Nor can it be forgotten that both before and after the two-year ban on aid contained in the Boland Amendment, Congress itself funded the contras. This year [1987] they have given the contras $100 million. The goal of the President in funding the contras is hardly incompatible with the majority view of Congress. This means that many in Congress do not view the President, North, or the CIA as having engaged in anything particularly evil. In fact, they were guilty at most of an excess of patriotism.

A Surface Investigation

The consensus regarding Nicaragua is part of a larger consensus among elites on the necessity of preventing or "rolling back" communism. This consensus insures that the damage from Iran-contragate will be limited. As the editors of *Monthly Review* recently stated, this "global counter-revolutionary policy and role . . . have dominated every government since the Second World War." In his book *The CIA: A Forgotten History*, William Blum documents CIA interventions in 49 countries since the end of World War II. Many of us are familiar with the most well known of these, e.g., the Congo, Chile, Guatemala, Iran, Jamaica, Grenada, El Salvador.

This policy on the need to prevent and defeat national liberation struggles and struggles for self-determination limits the investigation in Washington merely to addressing some of the excesses of the policy and not the policy itself. It also means that institutions that carry out the program must be left substantially intact. This is why, for example, Senator [David] Boren insisted that there was no systematic institutional involvement by the CIA. It is

why the Tower Commission concluded that their "review validates the current National Security Council system." Indeed, a lesson may have been learned from Watergate: a lesson about how far and deep an investigation should be permitted to go.

The Reagan Administration, however, has given us something different from what we had under [President] Carter. Reagan has returned us to the period of the 60s and 70s when covert operations were the normal course. We had hoped that at least the worst excesses of that period were over after the revelations regarding the attempts to kill Fidel Castro and the successful effort to overthrow [Salvador] Allende. Alfonso Chardy of the *Miami Herald* has documented 50 such actions happening worldwide. Some of these have been exposed such as the efforts to support the rebels in Afghanistan, Angola, Cambodia, and, of course, Nicaragua. Others are less well-known and include operations in Ethiopia, Chad, Guatemala, El Salvador, and even the United States. Through the Office of Public Diplomacy, the NSC conducted a three-year propaganda campaign to influence media coverage including so-called leaks that reflected badly on Nicaragua. The CIA, FBI [Federal Bureau of Investigation], and NSC have also cooperated to spy on and gather intelligence on those opposing Administration policies.

In addition to increased reliance on covert operations, this Administration has used the NSC to carry out some of these operations. In the *Miami Herald* article, Chardy stated that the NSC has engaged in at least ten such covert operations. We cannot look at the Nicaragua policy in isolation. It is part of a larger global policy to push back revolutionary change, and that policy is carried out covertly by the NSC to keep it hidden from public debate. Activities undertaken by the NSC have the added benefit of avoiding Congressional reporting requirements placed on the CIA. President Reagan has truly established a government of the Executive, by the Executive, and for the Executive.

Grave Dangers

The Iran-contragate scandal demonstrates that there has been a serious erosion of Congressional authority and an unwarrented enhancement of Presidential powers contrary to the balance of powers mandated by the Constitution. The increased power of the Executive, a power exercised in secret without either Congressional accountability or public debate, poses grave dangers to people abroad and Americans at home.

We have already seen the damage this power can cause abroad. The dead and injured in Nicaragua, the Middle East, and elsewhere are a tragic testament to the costs of this policy. Although we are faced with a constitutional crisis far greater than that demonstrated by Watergate, we must not lose sight of the larger context of illegality in which this particular crisis is set: the United States' policy of crushing governments and movements around the world that seek to determine their own economic and political destiny.

In the Reagan Administration's secret team, we have seen this policy carried to its logical extreme. Not only does such a policy violate international norms of justice, but increasingly it threatens the rule of law and the preservation of constitutional democracy at home. A plan for martial law and the detention of American citizens in the event of widespread internal opposition to U.S. intervention in the Third World—a plan apparently drafted by Colonel North—shows just how dangerous the present crisis is.

"A non-democratic, criminal policy abroad bends democracy at home and leaves us all open to greater danger."

We have already seen the effects of this covert war policy at home. FBI spying upon and disrupting the work of individuals and groups that oppose U.S. actions in Central America are again commonplace. Ideas that differ from those held by the current Administration are suppressed, and speakers from other countries who might hold alternative views are denied entrance visas. The policy has created millions of immigrants—particularly from Central America—who receive arbitrary, discriminatory, and unlawful treatment in the United States; and recently, what appear to be death squads similar to those operating in El Salvador have surfaced in Los Angeles—their targets: Central Americans who oppose U.S. intervention in that region. A non-democratic, criminal policy abroad bends democracy at home and leaves us all open to greater danger.

Hopefully, the Iran-contragate scandal will embolden the American people to address the real issues of concern. While there is general consensus in Congress and among elites over the aims of U.S. foreign policy, there is no consensus among the American people. The majority, for example, have opposed aid to the contras throughout the period in question. And there are even disagreements within Congress and among the elites over the extent of Congressional involvement in making foreign policy and in the accountability of the Executive Branch. The scandal is deepening in these divisions. Laws have been broken, the Constitution disregarded, Congress has been snubbed, and the American people ignored. This is an opportune moment to begin making democracy work.

Michael Ratner is the legal director for the Center for Constitutional Rights.

"Most of the legal arguments used to attack the administration are specious."

The Iran-Contra Affair Was Not Illegal

David B. Rivkin Jr.

In the aftermath of the Iran-Contra congressional hearings, the legal issues surrounding the executive branch's policies have assumed overriding importance.

It has now become an article of faith that laws were broken in the process of steering private and third-party support to the Nicaraguan freedom fighters and in the selling of arms to Iran. Specifically, it is posited that the Iranian arms sales were carried out in a way that violated the statutory prescriptions dealing with intelligence oversight, as well as the Arms Export Control Act. The support for the Contras effected through Lt. Col. Oliver North's "enterprise" is alleged to have run afoul of the third permutation of the Boland Amendment (Boland III).

More generally, opponents of the president's policies claim that the failure of the executive branch to consult with Congress, the administration's efforts to carry out policies through private channels, and the falsehoods deliberately proferred by certain administration members, when responding to congressional inquiries, raised profound constitutional concerns. In addition, there have been allegations that various participants in the Iran-Contra affair may have violated the Neutrality Act and committed sundry crimes ranging from defrauding the government and obstructing justice to conspiring to violate as yet unspecified laws.

Overall, the whole affair has turned into a lawyer's dream. Indeed, rightly or wrongly, technical legality seems to have become a major litmus test by which to judge the acceptability of any foreign policy venture. Unfortunately, most of the legal arguments used to attack the administration are specious in nature and represent a thinly disguised attempt to settle policy differences under the guise of a legal debate.

One of the key legal arguments raised by critics of the administration concerns its alleged violations of Boland III. This claim, however, is unpersuasive. Boland III states that "no funds available" to the CIA [Central Intelligence Agency], the Department of Defense, "or any other agency or entity of the United States involved in intelligence activities" could be used to support the Contras. Despite the seemingly sweeping language of this provision, it was attached to two congressional acts that, by their own terms, applied only to certain specific agencies of the U.S. government. The National Security Council (NSC) was *not* one of these agencies. Thus, on its face Boland III did not apply to the NSC. This argument was cogently presented in the now-famous memorandum by the President's Intelligence Oversight Board (PIOB), which prompted savage personal attacks by the anti-Reagan forces against the memorandum's author, Bretton G. Sciaroni.

The Intelligence Community

Several other reasons suggest that the NSC was not covered by Boland III. The amendment referred to "any agency or entity of the United States involved in intelligence activities." Commenting on this point, the PIOB noted that an identical formulation had been employed in "successive intelligence authorization acts dating from 1978 to the present," and, on all of these occasions referred only to members of the "intelligence community," rather than to the entire U.S. government. The PIOB then observed that Congress has been well aware of the concept of the "intelligence community"—a group of government agencies that routinely carry out intelligence activities—and argued that the language of the amendment just as the language of prior intelligence authorization acts, referred only to the constituent members of that community. In contrast,

David B. Rivkin Jr., "Were Any Laws Broken in the Iran-Contra Affair?" This article appeared in the November 1987 issue and is reprinted with permission from *The World & I,* a publication of the Washington Times Corporation. Copyright 1987.

the NSC has never been considered a member of the intelligence community—a conclusion that is corroborated by the fact that Sec. 3.4 (f) of Executive Order No. 12333, issued by President Reagan in December 1981, listed the members of the intelligence community, and the NSC was not among them.

Moreover, as a part of the Executive Office of the President, the NSC has never been subject to congressional regulation.

This fact was acknowledged by Congress. Thus, numerous members of Congress concluded in 1985, that Boland III did not extend to the NSC. For example, in August 1985, Rep. George Brown (D-California), a member of the House Intelligence Committee and an opponent of Contra aid, observed: "If the president wants to use the NSC to operate a war in Nicaragua, I don't think there is any way we can control it."

Faulty Interpretation

Despite the compelling evidence that Boland III was narrow in scope, the proponents of its "broad interpretation" have advanced a range of arguments to the contrary. First, they argue that when Congressman Boland, the amendment's sponsor, described Boland III on the House floor, he claimed that the "provision ends U.S. support for the war in Nicaragua," thereby indicating that the amendment's jurisdictional ambit encompassed the NSC.

Boland, however, made no special mention of the amendment's applicability to the NSC. If that, indeed, was his intention, it should have been clearly expressed. This clarity would have been all the more imperative, since, as Congressman Boland was well aware, restricting the foreign policy operations of the NSC would have had important constitutional ramifications.

It is also a well-established precept of statutory interpretation that statements by members of Congress cannot override the plain meaning of the statutory text. Thus, even if Congressman Boland's remarks on the House floor are to be construed as expressing his belief that the entire federal government, including the NSC, was covered by the amendment, since the amendment, as enacted, does not so state, his remarks are irrelevant.

"The NSC has never been considered a member of the intelligence community."

It also has been suggested that if not the letter, then at least the "spirit" of the amendment applied to the NSC, and barred all activities by NSC officials in support of the Nicaraguan democratic resistance. In fact, much discussion concerning the spirit of Boland took place during the hearings. But this claim is hollow.

In general, statutes purporting to regulate "gray" constitutional areas involving the overlapping responsibilities of coordinate branches of government are to be construed narrowly. Additionally, a "spirit" of a given statute is usually established by examining the underlying "general congressional intent." In this case, given all the congressional flip-flops on Contra aid, reflected in contradictory Boland Amendments, one would have to be a psychiatrist to fathom the spirit of Boland III.

The proponents of the "broad reading" argue that the "narrow" interpretation of Boland would make the amendment ineffectual. As asserted by Senator George Mitchell (D-Maine) during the hearings, if Boland III applied only to the members of the intelligence community, Contra support operations could have been legally orchestrated by the Agriculture Department.

This *reductio ad absurdum* approach is unconvincing. A statute often fails to accomplish what its congressional drafters intended.

Furthermore, as Gordon Crovitz argued in the *Wall Street Journal*, there is considerable evidence that Congress deliberately drafted all of the Boland Amendments in such a way as to preserve the ability of the president to continue supporting the Contras. This was in part to avoid a bruising confrontation with the White House and to preserve some vestige of presidential flexibility.

Once the fact of the Iran-Contra connection became public, Congress, irrespective of its original views on the issue, could not resist the temptation to attack the administration. To a certain degree, this change of heart on the part of Congress is attributable to the disjointed and melodramatic way in which the affair was handled by the administration. It can be argued that had the White House issued a cogent and strong defense of its policy, congressional and media attitudes might have evolved quite differently.

Additionally, much has been made of Robert McFarlane's reassurance to Congress that the NSC was fully complying with Boland III. It is clear, however, that McFarlane's comments pertained to the political impact of Boland III, rather than to its statutory scope. In any case, his statement did not constitute a considered legal opinion.

A Flawed Premise

Lurking behind the "battle of interpretations" over Boland III are some fundamental constitutional issues that have so far received scant notice. To begin with, there are some questions about the constitutionality of even the "narrow" reading of the amendment. The courts have traditionally recognized presidential preeminence in foreign affairs. They have also held that the congressional power of the purse is not absolute and that Congress may not attain indirectly, through the appropriation process, an outcome that would be constitutionally proscribed if it were sought directly. Relevant case law also distinguishes between withholding funds, a generally permissible congressional activity, and placing restrictions on appropriated funds. The latter approach is constitutionally suspect.

In the past, various presidents chose to disregard restrictions attached to appropriations bills. The question in such situations had been whether the outcome that Congress was trying to effect was constitutionally within the orbit of congressional powers. For example, congressional efforts to cut off funds for the war in Vietnam, while perhaps erroneous as a matter of policy, were constitutionally proper, deriving from Congress' power to declare and terminate wars. In contrast, however, Congress has no constitutional authority to prescribe what causes or movements the president can support.

"Congress has no constitutional authority to prescribe what causes or movements the president can support."

In a somewhat broader context, congressional advocates chastise Reagan for violating the principle of codetermination that envisions [the] executive and Congress functioning as coequal foreign policymakers. There is no doubt that both the president and Congress possess vast foreign affairs power. It is also true that, in comparison to the domestic sphere, where the executive and legislative roles are delineated fairly well, the division of labor in foreign policy is much less clear. Some of the congressional powers overlap the executive's, producing what the courts have referred to as the "zone of twilight." In fact, the Constitution provides for a certain inherent tension between the branches of government. At times, such tension has erupted into battles between the executive and Congress over the domination of foreign policy. Although on some specific foreign policy matters the delineation of congressional and executive roles may present problems, in foreign affairs generally, executive preeminence is beyond dispute.

Many scholars also believe that the president's authority in the foreign affairs area does not stem solely from the constitutional text. This view was eloquently articulated by Justice Sutherland in the famous case *United States v. Curtis-Wright Export Corp.* [in 1936, which acknowledged a broad presidential power to make executive agreements with other nations]. Sutherland argued that the Declaration of Independence gave sovereignty,

originally vested in the British Crown, to the colonies in their collective capacity rather than to individual states. Subsequently, the sovereignty vested in the United Colonies passed on to the "a more perfect Union" established by the Constitution. In contrast to the domestic powers of the federal government, which were carved out of the powers previously held by the states and had to be carefully delineated, the framers of the Constitution apparently did not foresee any need to detail foreign affairs powers available to the federal government.

Congress Ill-Suited

It is significant, however, that Article II of the Constitution states that "the Executive power shall be vested in a President of the United States of America." Insofar as the power to conduct foreign policy has traditionally been considered executive in nature, this clause can be construed to imply that the president possesses all foreign affairs-related powers available to the federal government except as otherwise provided in the Constitution for Congress and the courts.

Constitutional factors aside, on practical grounds, Congress is clearly ill suited for genuine codetermination. Such factors as leaks, breakdown of the congressional seniority system, excessive responsiveness to lobbies and pressure groups, as well as a discernable tendency to avoid hard choices and opt for compromise solutions, greatly hamper congressional effectiveness in conducting American foreign policy. The ongoing congressional handwringing over reflagging Kuwaiti tankers is an excellent example. Most members of Congress did not have the courage either to oppose the initiative outright or to support it unequivocally, calling instead for further delays and studies.

Claims that using private funds and channels to conduct U.S. foreign policy is illegal are also without merit. There is nothing in the Constitution, statutes, or case law that prohibits the president from using private individuals to assist in various foreign policy ventures. Critics conveniently forget that many presidents, beginning with George Washington, used private individuals to conduct sensitive foreign policy or intelligence missions. The practice of using private-sector funding is also not new. For example, in the aftermath of World War II, the AFL-CIO [American Federation of Labor—Congress of Industrial Organizations], with the knowledge of the executive branch, raised a large amount of money from wealthy Americans. . . . These funds were funneled to the fledgling European trade unions to counteract Soviet funding.

Moreover, congressional micro-management of foreign policy is, to a large extent, responsible for the executive's inclination occasionally to "privatize" U.S. foreign policy. Congressional insistence that no foreign aid funds can be reprogrammed without congressional approval forced President Carter to seek funding from the Saudis for Somalia during the 1978 Ogaden war. Interestingly, in that instance, Congress did not oppose the aid; the congressional machinery simply could not react in a timely fashion.

The proponents of the "broad" interpretation seem to have casually ignored the rather startling constitutional implications of their argument: Insofar as Boland III refers to the funds "available" to the government, not only was the NSC covered by the amendment, but expenditure for the Contras of private or third-party funds raised by U.S. government officials would be unlawful. Commenting on this issue, [former Senator] Walter Mondale opined that any funds raised by federal officials are really federal funds. The logical corollary of this argument is that should North ever organize a Boy Scout raffle, the money raised, instead of going to charity, should be deposited in the U.S. Treasury.

Furthermore, to argue that Congress can ever preclude the president or his agents from soliciting foreign or private funds implies that Congress can prescribe our entire foreign policy agenda. Undoubtedly, such an outcome would be constitutionally deficient.

Some have tried to dispose of this problem by claiming that while the amendment might not have prohibited the president from soliciting funds for the Contras or providing other forms of support, it did bar his subordinates from engaging in these activities. This argument ignores the fact that a president does not even place his own phone calls.

Intelligence Oversight

In the last two decades, an elaborate system of intelligence oversight has sprung up. The Hughes-Ryan Amendment requires a presidential finding (essentially a formal decision by the president) before funds can be spent by the CIA on any covert activity. The Intelligence Oversight Act of 1980 provides for the "timely" notification of Congress by the Director of Central Intelligence (DCI) of such findings. In letter, Hughes-Ryan applies only to the CIA, but Executive Order 12333 lists a number of other entities of the intelligence community that may become involved in covert action only if the president so determines.

This order further specifies that such determinations are treatable as a Hughes-Ryan finding, and as such, are reportable to Congress by the DCI. Meanwhile, the Arms Export Control Act generally requires that a valid reexport license be issued whenever a third country intends to sell U.S.-origin arms and that Congress be notified whenever such arms are valued in excess of a certain amount. It it this elaborate set of legal structures that the Iranian arms deal and North's "Contra enterprise"

have allegedly violated.

Specifically, with regard to the November 1985 arms shipment, with which the CIA was involved, no finding was drafted until after the arms had already been delivered. Furthermore, two shipments to Iran by the Israelis in the summer of 1985 reportedly involved arms that the U.S. had previously sold to Israel. On both occasions, U.S. approval was sought and obtained. However, no valid reexport licenses were issued by the U.S. government, and Congress was not notified of the reexports.

"Claims that using private funds and channels to conduct U.S. foreign policy is illegal are also without merit."

If U.S. approval of such Israeli activities is to be construed as participation in a covert operation, rather than as an arms reexport, then appropriate findings should have been promulgated. Apparently, this was not done. Nor was a written finding ever drafted to cover the activities of the NSC in support of the Contras. Moreover, no notification of the findings covering subsequent Iran arms shipments was given to Congress until after the Iranian operation was disclosed by a Middle Eastern newspaper. Thus, it is argued that the administration failed to comply with both of the overriding principles of the intelligence oversight system, insofar as it did not issue appropriate written findings, and did not notify Congress about the ongoing covert activities.

Upon closer examination, however, the legal case against the administration for allegedly violating the intelligence oversight procedures and the Arms Export Control Act appears to be less than airtight. First of all, it can be argued that the president, by approving the Israeli reexports of arms to Iran, chose to treat these activities as a joint covert operation, placing Israel and the NSC outside the ambit of the Arms Export Control Act.

Second, with regard to the Intelligence Oversight Act, it is not clear that the president's failure to inform Congress about the relevant findings until eighteen months after the Iranian initiative began constitutes an "untimely" notification.

Concern About Leaks

Although the view that an eighteen-month delay in notifying Congress is timely may strike a layman as odd, it is clear that "timely" is a term of art. It was inserted in the statutory language to allow the president requisite flexibility in carrying out extremely sensitive covert operations. Indications in the legislative history of the Intelligence Oversight

Act suggest that at the time it was enacted, no protracted delays in notification were envisioned. But no conclusive evidence demonstrates that any fixed deadline for notification was established.

Unquestionably, the failure to promulgate the requisite finding in advance of the November 1985 shipment constitutes a technical violation of the Hughes-Ryan Amendment. Yet it appears that corrective actions were seasonably taken, since the finding covering the shipment was drafted within a few days after the shipment.

Assuming *arguendo* that NSC activities supporting the 1985 Israeli shipments and the Contra operations merit the designation of covert action, since Executive Order 12333 does not list the NSC as a member of the intelligence community, the president was not obligated to make a formal finding prior to directing the NSC to proceed. Furthermore, even if such a determination was made by the president, since the NSC is not a member of the intelligence community, such a finding, if any, would not be subject to the Hughes-Ryan Amendment and to the reporting requirements of the Oversight Act.

It should also be recognized that the administration's reticence to brief Congress on the Iranian initiative was prompted by its legitimate concern about leaks. Damaging leaks about the *Achille Lauro* incident and the 1985 U.S.-Egyptian-Sudanese plans concerning Libya are excellent examples. Moreover, the president is acutely aware that, leaks aside, Congress may decide to declassify information regarding any pending covert operation. While Congress has never exercised this authority, it still exists as a possibility to be reckoned with.

As a more fundamental point, in many respects, the 1980 Intelligence Oversight Act is riddled with ambiguities and loopholes. For instance, arguably the act acknowledges the right of the president to withhold certain information from Congress indefinitely. It does not, however, specify what these matters might be.

It is also clear that the act does *not* require disclosure of secret foreign policy ventures to Congress. An operation such as the "opening" to the People's Republic of China, carried out in secrecy by President Nixon and Secretary Kissinger, is a perfect example. Yet the act does not even address the issue of "how much covert action is enough" to make a foreign policy operation reportable to Congress. In fact, in the present case, a good argument can be made that the Iranian arms deals were primarily a foreign policy operation and not a covert action.

Inherent Power To Defend

The Neutrality Act of 1794 generally bars hostile actions originating from U.S. soil against any nation, unless and until Congress has issued a declaration of war against that nation. It has been suggested that the act proscribes the actions undertaken by North and other members of the enterprise in support of the Nicaraguan freedom fighters, irrespective of whether or not such actions were approved by the president. Some pundits noted that in the past individuals were prosecuted under the act for activities conducted with apparent executive authorization. The last such prosecution occurred in 1806.

This argument is specious. First, as Professor John Norton Moore argues, Nicaragua has been engaged in an armed aggression against its neighbors. This action entitles the United States as a matter of international law—under the UN Charter and the Rio Treaty—to engage in actions designed to repel the aggression. Moreover, under Article VI of the Constitution, the Rio Treaty is the supreme law of the land. Thus, as a matter of U.S. domestic law, even in the absence of congressional authorization, the president is entitled to take reasonable steps to repel Nicaraguan aggression. The Rio Treaty aside, the president is generally believed to possess inherent power to defend the United States against aggression.

"A good argument can be made that the Iranian arms deals were primarily a foreign policy operation and not a covert action."

Second, the uncritical invocation of the Neutrality Act ignores the profound change in the nature of warfare since 1794. No formal declaration of war was ever made. In fact, the Neutrality Act argument, if taken to its logical conclusion, suggests that any covert action, whether or not reported to Congress, constitutes a violation of the Neutrality Act.

A modification of the Neutrality Act argument propounded by some pundits posits that although the congressional declaration of war may no longer be required for the Neutrality Act not to be violated, Congress has to indicate that "a state of peace" does not exist between the United States and the country concerned. In the present case, however, congressional actions vis-á-vis Nicaragua—Boland III notwithstanding—clearly provided such an indication.

Numerous other allegations have been made that various participants in the enterprise engaged in tax crimes, lied to government officials and to Congress, obstructed justice, conspired to defraud the government, and conspired to violate the Arms Export Control Act. Yet the facts that have emerged so far seem to suggest that the legal case, at least against North and [Admiral John] Poindexter, is rather weak. Lying to Congress may be ethically objectionable, but it does not, however, constitute a crime, unless one is testifying under oath. While there is a general statutory proscription against providing false information to government officials, North's misstatements to various government officials can be justified by the so-called need-to-know principle.

No Obstruction of Justice

The obstruction of justice charges are valid only if one assumes that North and Poindexter destroyed the relevant evidence while they were aware of a criminal investigation into the affair. It can be argued that this was not the case. The early efforts by the attorney general to look into the Iran-Contra matter could reasonably be construed as an informal fact-finding mission for the president, rather than as a criminal investigation. Likewise, alleged efforts at a cover-up by other government officials, though indicative of poor judgment, do not amount to an obstruction of justice, since no criminal investigation was either taking place or could be foreseen at the time.

Since the so-called residuals generated from the sale of arms to Iran arguably did not belong to the U.S. government, it is difficult to understand the basis of any claims that the U.S. government was defrauded in the process.

The conspiracy claim is also based on the proposition that the activities of the "enterprise" were barred by Boland III. If the amendment did not apply to the NSC and did not proscribe private fund-raising for the Contras, there appears to be no basis for any conspiracy claims. Since the president arguably opted to waive the Arms Export Control Act by designating U.S. involvement with Israeli arms shipments as a covert action, it is unclear how the individuals could have conspired to violate a law that did not apply to this situation.

"Ironically, a credible legal justification could well have been developed to enable the president to proceed with the policies."

As far as the tax crimes allegedly committed by [fundraiser Carl] Channel and others are concerned, even assuming that these allegations are true, there is no evidence that North instigated such activities. Moreover, under the general tenets of agency law, principals usually are not liable for the criminal conduct of their agents, unless they participated in or encouraged such conduct. In fact, upon reflection, the only action taken by North and Poindexter that does constitute a technical violation was North's acceptance of the security system for his house in Virginia.

One is left to wonder whether the interests of justice are well served by prosecuting government officials on such a flimsy basis. Such prosecutions, if carried out—whether or not individuals are incarcerated—are likely to have a chilling impact on the future foreign policy operations of the executive branch.

Public vs. Private Policy

A strong sentiment has been expressed by many members of Congress that, somehow, it is both immoral and unconstitutional to pursue a course that differs from one's publicly articulated policy. In fact, some pundits . . . have used the Iran-Contra hearings as an occasion to renew calls to outlaw all covert actions.

A view has also been expressed that any paramilitary support for resistance movements in the Third World should not be treated as a covert operation and, instead, should be openly debated in Congress. It is also claimed that insofar as the American people have failed to back overwhelmingly the administration's policy toward Nicaragua, supporting the Contras was improper. Yet, confusion and ambiguity frequently accompany aggression in the contemporary world, and democracies are rarely presented with a clear-cut challenge. Thus, the American public is often not aware of the magnitude of the threat we face.

Clearly, some legal and policy mistakes were made in the way in which the administration's policies toward Iran and Nicaragua were executed. There is no indication that serious legal advice was sought and obtained at the time these policies were formulated. Ironically, a credible legal justification could well have been developed to enable the president to proceed with the policies. This never took place. In fact, it can be argued that if the administration staked out a strong and forthright legal position even as late as November 1986 and justified its policies toward Iran and Nicaragua on solid constitutional grounds, Congress and the media might have treated the whole affair differently. Instead, the apparent panic, disarray, and confusion at the White House, as well as public efforts by various high-ranking administration officials to distance themselves from the president's policies, have greatly emboldened Congress to go for the jugular.

All of this suggests that when the current political passions subside, the most lasting legacy of the Contra affair is likely to be its role as a case study for the Kennedy School of Government on how crises should not be handled.

David B. Rivkin Jr. is an attorney in Washington, DC who writes on defense and foreign affairs topics.

"The Iran-contra committees had neither the instinct nor the resolve to pursue Presidential wrongdoing to its logical end."

The Iran-Contra Committees Favored the President

The Progressive

The Iran-contra miniseries made good theater but bad politics. It entertained and at times enthralled, but it did not enlighten. And in the end, it made a mockery of itself and a sham of Congressional power.

Rarely, perhaps once in a decade, Congress shakes off its habitual lethargy and rises to question the excesses of the Presidency. Faintly aware that the constitutional arrangements have fallen into disuse and disrepair, the Legislative branch tries to apply the brakes to the runaway Executive.

This time, Congress put up even less of a fight than usual. Content to pursue individual malfeasance, blind to institutional venality, the Iran-contra committees staged one of the fluffiest political dramas in memory. Wrists were slapped, the naughty were lectured, but the full and frightening dimensions of the scandal went unexplored, and the political and ideological roots remain intact.

Unlike Sam Ervin's Watergate panel [in 1973] . . . , the Iran-contra committees had neither the instinct nor the resolve to pursue Presidential wrongdoing to its logical end. And unlike Frank Church's CIA [Central Intelligence Agency] probe eleven years ago, the Iran-contra committees refused to delve into the shady and wholly undemocratic world of covert action. The committees have not drafted bills of impeachment, nor have they considered outlawing—or even severely curtailing—covert actions.

The abysmal failure of the hearings carries with it a terrible human cost. . . . The U.S. Government will be free to conduct a great variety of covert wars in the future, so long as a few "trustworthy" Congressional leaders are cut in on the deal.

Congress passed up an extraordinary opportunity to expose the darker side of the Reagan Administration. But more than that, it missed a historic opportunity to rein in the Presidency and restore a semblance of decency and democracy to American foreign policy. Its failure is the country's loss and the whole world's misfortune.

Black Glove of US Intervention

At bottom, the investigating committees accepted what they should have been questioning: the necessity of U.S. covert action around the globe. Virtually every witness, from General Richard Secord and Lieutenant Colonel Oliver North to Secretary of State George Shultz and [then] Defense Secretary Caspar Weinberger, stressed the indispensability of covert action. Not a single member of the committees challenged the assumption that the United States should be engaged in that ugly business.

"By their very nature, covert operations are a lie," North said, and he was absolutely right. But no one on the committees dared even to question whether operations grounded in deceit are so antidemocratic at their core that they should be outlawed.

"I think it is very important for the American people to understand that this is a dangerous world, that we live at risk," North said on his first day of testimony by way of justifying covert activity.

Respresentative after Representative, Senator after Senator, Democrat after Republican parroted North on the need for covert action in a "complex" or "dangerous" world. Whenever those code words were uttered, it was safe to conclude that a justification for antidemocratic acts was to follow, one that invariably accepted the premise that the American people—and even a majority of their elected officials—are not to be informed of some of the most far-reaching actions undertaken by their Government.

No one pointed out that covert actions are seldom, if ever, carried out to protect the United States from imminent danger. They are, instead, the black glove of U.S. intervention. A list of U.S. covert actions is a record of bloody intrusions into the affairs of sovereign nations: Iran in 1953, Guatemala in 1954, the Congo in 1960, Cuba in 1961, Indonesia in 1965, Vietnam in the 1960s, Chile in 1973, Nicaragua in the 1980s. None of these countries threatened the United States.

Nor was there more than fleeting mention of the fact that most covert operations are kept secret *only* from the American people. When Cambodia was ravaged by "secret" U.S. bombing in the Johnson and Nixon Administrations, the Cambodians certainly knew about the bombings, and so did the Vietnamese, the Russians, the Chinese, and the Thais, from whose air bases American B-52s were launched. Only the American public was deliberately kept in the dark about its Goverment's nefarious acts.

"Congress failed, in part, because it was reluctant to recognize, examine, and correct its own mistakes that helped lay the groundwork for the scandal."

Similarly, the Iran-contra arms conspirators did not hesitate to share their intrigues with foreign governments and international drifters, while going to extreme lengths of concealment and deception to keep the public, the Congress, and even their own colleagues in the Executive branch uninformed.

More than a decade ago, the late Senator Frank Church of Idaho conducted searching hearings exposing the nature of covert actions, but memory fades quickly on Capitol Hill. In today's Congress, the doubts have been silenced, the problems overlooked.

"It is, as you said, a dangerous world, and we must be able to conduct covert actions, as every member of this panel has said," Lee Hamilton, Democrat of Indiana, who headed the House Iran-Contra Committee, acknowledged in his closing remarks to North. And Hamilton was relatively tough on North. Other members fawned on him in a repulsive orgy of obsequiousness.

Questioning Means, Not Ends

The unanimous endorsement of covert action points up one of the major failings of the hearings. If everyone accepts the premise that the United States must behave in ways that cannot stand the light of day, it is hardly surprising that fundamental questions about such behavior will go unaddressed. All that the investigators left on their agenda was "the means employed," as Representative Hamilton put it.

The means were faulty, according to the committees, because the Reagan Administration did not follow the standard procedure for covert actions. It did not submit a finding to the leaders of the Senate and House Intelligence Committees who, by statute, must be notified. At most, the committees were suggesting that eight members of Congress be notified, and perhaps as few as four. No one seemed to harbor any doubts about the propriety of having four or eight out of 535 elected members of the House and Senate make decisions on whether the United States should foment war or not. They just wanted to join the cabal.

Senator George Mitchell, Democrat of Maine, scored a debating point with Oliver North by showing how undemocratic the Marine officer's approach was. If the only check on the President was whether the people approved of his actions, and if the people were kept in the dark about his actions, then the people would have no basis for checking the President, Mitchell noted.

What Mitchell failed to address was that the people still have no basis for checking the President. Notifying a handful of Congressional leaders, and swearing them to secrecy, doesn't solve the problem.

But because the committees refused even to consider the legitimacy of covert action, they were in no position to recommend any sweeping changes in the way the United States conducts its foreign policy. It was much safer simply to scold North, Poindexter, [Elliott] Abrams and [Edwin] Meese for their lies and deceptions, or to worry about money stolen by middlemen or spent on snow tires, or to dwell on the White House intrigue between Cabinet members and the National Security Council.

"I haven't seen anything radically wrong with the system, but there was something wrong with the people," said Senator Warren Rudman, Republican of New Hampshire. A few months earlier, the Reagan-appointed Tower Commission reached virtually the same conclusion.

Congress at Fault

Congress failed, in part, because it was reluctant to recognize, examine, and correct its own mistakes that helped lay the groundwork for the scandal. It must "share the blame" for the Iran-contra fiasco, though not in the sense intended by Lieutenant Colonel Oliver North, Admiral John Poindexter, and their faithful Republican chorus on the committees, all of whom would cheerfully abolish Congress if they had the choice.

Congress's first and most basic error was to enact the National Security Act of 1947, the legislative foundation for the national security state that was fashioned to wage Cold War against the Soviet Union.

Had the National Security Act been accurately labeled, it would have been called An Act to

Facilitate the Expansion of the American Empire and Diminish Democracy Within the United States. It was the National Security Act that established the Central Intelligence Agency and the National Security Council, and in doing so effectively transferred all control over foreign policy from the Congress to the Presidency. If Congress had any gumption and any real commitment to constitutional democracy, it would hold hearings now on repealing the National Security Act.

Other mistakes have been more recent, chief among them not taking a decisive stand against U.S. meddling in Nicaragua's affairs. Congress should have strengthened the Boland Amendment and insisted that it be followed; instead, it was diluted by Congress and flouted by the Administration.

After the first Boland Amendment was passed—and more than two years before the Iran scandal broke—the press carried reports of Oliver North aiding the contras from his position on the National Security Council staff. It was common knowledge in Washington. Congress should have held immediate hearings on the matter and should have enacted clear, airtight legislation that would have prohibited any U.S. agency or official from assisting the contras.

Nothing of the sort occurred. Members of Lee Hamilton's House Intelligence Committee talked privately with North and accepted his patently false assurances that he was not aiding the contras. Perhaps a few members of the committee were actually naive enough to believe what they were told. The rest eagerly accepted what they wanted to hear. Congress returned to the issue [in 1987] . . . only because there was a whiff of truly unacceptable Administration behavior—the clandestine sale of arms to the regime of the Ayatollah Khomeini.

Capitulation on the issue of the contras was perhaps the most disgraceful display the Iran-contra committees put on. The Democratic leadership allowed North and other witnesses to prattle on with their lurid propaganda about the contras. Lie upon lie was fed to the American public on national television, and no member of the committees dared take the microphone to refute them.

"The staffs of the committees were hopelessly biased in favor of the contras and covert actions."

Not a single Senator or Representative stood up to set the record straight: to demonstrate that the contra leadership is composed largely of members of the late dictator Anastasio Somoza's dreaded National Guard; to list the murders, tortures, and other actrocities committed by the contras. No one took issue when North, Poindexter, and other witnesses ceaselessly referred to the contras as "freedom fighters." It was as if U.S. aid to this brutal band of counterrevolutionaries had ceased to be an issue. Everyone agreed that they were the good guys.

Even Edward Boland, the Massachusetts Democrat who sponsored the effort to halt U.S. military assistance to the contras, gave a bloodless and legalistic account of the amendment that bears his name, avoiding all moral and political considerations and sticking to the formal question of whether the statute was violated.

Senator Daniel Inouye, the Hawaii Democrat who chaired the Senate committee, was the only member to defend opposition to the contras, and he did so in terms the verged on the apologetic.

"Ladies and gentlemen and Colonel North, I voted against aid to the contras. I did so not as a communist, I did so not as an agent of the K.G.B. [Soviet intelligence agency]. . . . I did so because I was firmly convinced that to follow the path or the course that was laid down by the Reagan proposal would certainly and inevitably lead to a point where young men and women of the United States would have to be sent into the conflict."

That Inouye felt compelled to deny being a communist shows how far to the Right the hearings had lurched. Thirty-five years after the heyday of McCarthyism, its noxious effects still linger.

Cowed into submission by North's popularity, the Democrats ceded the issue of aid to the contras. And the Republicans, led by Representative Henry Hyde of Illinois and Senator Orrin Hatch of Utah, made the most of it.

Questions Not Asked

The Democrats bear the responsibility for allowing the hearings to turn into a contra pep rally. They bent over backward to put their most "moderate" members on the panel, deliberately excluding those who had been most outspoken in their opposition to U.S. intervention in Central America. Senators Edward Kennedy, John Kerry, and Christopher Dodd were not invited to participate in the hearings, nor were Representatives Henry B. Gonzalez or Ron Dellums. All in all, some two-thirds of the members of the investigating committees were on record as supporting the contras.

To make matters worse, the staffs of the committees were hopelessly biased in favor of the contras and covert actions, as *In These Times* has reported. The chief investigator on the Senate staff was Thomas Polgar, who had been the CIA station chief in Vietnam when Saigon fell. Another Senate investigator, Joel Lisker, had worked with none other than Oliver North in a March 1985 attempt to shuttle aid to the Nicaraguan contras. With the deck so stacked, the committees were in no position to deal out an aggressive inquiry.

Perhaps that is why the most sinister elements of the scandal scarcely received an airing. For months and months, information has accumulated implicating the contras and Reagan Administration officials in the illegal drug trade. One could have expected the Democrats to press the issue, but they did not.

The only member who addressed it head-on was Orrin Hatch, who asked, in his unctuous way, the following question of Oliver North:

"O.K., what about drug smuggling? There've been a lot of allegations thrown around that the contra resupply operation was involved in cocaine trafficking. A news program, over the weekend, suggested that Rob Owen, who testified earlier, was involved in drug smuggling. Now, is there any truth to that? Can you shed any light for us on that question?"

North: "Absolutely false. Mr. Owen is the last person, perhaps right beside me, that would ever be engaged in those kinds of activities and when Mr. Owen found any information pertaining to the possibility of involvement in drugs, he told me and I would tell the appropriate Federal authorities. And there were several of such instances. Absolutely false, Senator."

Case closed. Not another question about it. Two days later, a Senate subcommittee heard testimony that two CIA agents were involved in a contra guns-for-drugs operation, but no one on the Iran-contra panels seems to have taken notice.

"When the controversial issues arose, the committees ducked."

And when Jack Brooks, Democrat of Texas, the only member to take an appropriately contemptuous attitude toward the witnesses, tried to ask North about his involvement in a plan to declare martial law in the United States, he was cut off by North's attorney, Brendan Sullivan, and Senator Inouye upheld the objection: "May I most respectfully request that matter not be touched upon, at this stage. If we wish to get into this, I'm certain arrangements can be made for an executive session."

According to press accounts, this scheme involved nothing less than an attempt to nullify the Constitution, but Congress wouldn't let the American people hear the details.

Similarly, the entire subject of joint U.S.-Israel covert actions were deemed off limits. Though there were ample hints of a prominent Israeli role in the arms transfers to Iran and in the furtive assistance rendered to the contras, the details of various operations were discussed in executive session—if they were discussed at all. And the committees brooked no mention of potential problems that might flow from a supranational intelligence agency made up of the CIA and Israel's Mossad [secret service].

When the controversial issues arose, the committees ducked.

Authoritarianism

What made the Congressional abdication even more worrisome was the indication that Congress merely reflected a widespread drift toward authoritarianism—a drift that might have been identified in more candid times as a prelude to fascism.

Fawn Hall cast it in the simplest, most revealing terms: "Sometimes you have to go above the written law." That seemed to be the credo of the Reagan Administration, and especially of its national-security apparatus. The laws are there to be broken, particularly if they interfere with anything the Chief Executive and Commander-in-Chief wants done. No lie was too blatant, no deception too crude to be mobilized in defense of our leader.

"I didn't want to show Congress a single word about this whole thing," North said.

"My objective, all along, was to withhold from the Congress exactly what the NSC [National Security Council] staff was doing in carrying out the President's policy," Poindexter said. "I simply didn't want any outside interference."

These, to put it gently, are not democratic sentiments. They are the sentiments of the soldier determined to follow orders, and North and Poindexter are, after all, military men. Their martial attitudes are understandable, though they hardly rendered them fit to hold high civilian office. What was astonishing and distressing, however, was the popularity of their philosophy as articulated in the networks' gavel-to-gavel coverage.

North and, to a lesser extent, Poindexter tapped the most reactionary sentiments in the American body politic. People admired North not just for his military bearing, his chestful of medals, and the gap between his two front teeth, but because he was willing to get things done, no matter the cost, no matter the legality. And when Poindexter complained about the obstacles placed in his path by "outsiders"—he meant Congress—who couldn't sympathize? Democracy was slow and creaky; here were guys who could make the trains run on time. It was useful to have a bracing reminder that the American can-do attitude has it authoritarian overtones.

But it wasn't just the efficiency of the runaway NSC staff that people revered. It was their ideology. Their unblushing patriotism of the my-country-right-or-wrong variety, their gung-ho anticommunism, swept America off its feet, even as they admitted repeated and enthusiastic participation in falsehood.

Primitive chauvinism, the sway of ideology over fact, and the pursuit of an aggressive foreign policy are traditional elements of fascist doctrine. That such conduct could win the plaudits of the American public, however briefly, should disquiet all those who cherish democracy.

"Our Executive branch, containing only two elected officials accountable to the people, has enormous unchecked power."

Other seamy aspects of extreme rightist politics surfaced during the hearings. After Arthur Liman, the Democratic Senate investigators' lawyer, grilled General Richard Secord about his profiteering in the Iran-arms deals, the committees were swamped with anti-Semitic mail. And when Senator Inouye didn't bow deeply enough to North, racist calls directed toward Inouye rang in the Committees' offices.

"We received some calls in the committee and our offices over the last seventy-two hours of ugly ethnic slurs against our chairman, and other kinds of calls that were extraordinarily insulting to the members of this committee," Senator Rudman announced angrily during North's testimony.

Bigotry, too, is central to fascism, and its reappearance with the testimony of General Secord and Colonel North underscored how fundamentally reactionary their actions were. It also demonstrated that their ilk has a constituency in this country, and that the most virulent hostility to the democratic process always lurks just below the surface of American political life.

The surge of mass support for the NSC outlaws recalls a line from Shakespeare: "Now this ill-wresting world is grown so bad, mad slanderers by mad ears believed be."

Congress Too Weak

Congress was established as an equal branch of Government. It is equal no longer. It has allowed its powers to atrophy, and its will has run dry. Every constitutional duty that it has abandoned, the Executive has usurped.

This evolution belies the seventh-grade civics lessons about checks and balances that the Senators and Representatives were so prone to recite during the hearings. Despite their platitudes, the Executive runs the show—either in the form of a President who call the shots or, as in Ronald Reagan's case, in the form of a free-wheeling gang of meddlers and manipulators who manage to surround a feeble and feckless President.

For a putative democracy, that's not good news. Our Executive branch, containing only two elected officials accountable to the people, has enormous unchecked power. Behind our backs, it overthrows governments, assassinates foreign leaders, bombs foreign capitals, trains torturers, and conducts campaigns of economic or military sabotage. It can declare martial law and trample our Constitution, as this Administration has planned. And it holds in its hands the power to destroy the world on a moment's notice—all in the name of protecting national security at home and promoting democracy abroad.

For the first time in more than a decade, Congress had an occasion to intervene in that ruinous process, restore the constitutional balance, and return the United States to a more democratic structure. It had the opportunity to step back from covert actions and rethink an interventionist foreign policy. It had, in short, a chance to institute a safer and more just system.

But it was not willing to take that chance.

The Progressive *is a monthly leftist political journal.*

"The [Iran-contra] hearings were clearly calculated to criminalize executive foreign policies."

The Iran-Contra Committees Opposed the President

Dennis Teti

In 1877, a unanimous Congress passed a joint resolution requesting the Secretary of State to send a letter thanking two governments that had congratulated Congress on the centennial of America's independence. President Grant, ending his second term under a cloud of scandal, agreed with the sentiments in the resolution, but vetoed it on the grounds that the legislative branch had no authority over correspondence with foreign powers. The vetoed bill was returned to the Senate Foreign Relations Committee where it was never heard of again. Even during the age of congressional government, as Woodrow Wilson later described the second half of the 19th century, no one challenged the supremacy given by the Constitution to the president in the conduct of foreign affairs.

In the past 15 years, Congress has aggressively sought to wrest away the president's control. The War Powers Act, the Clark Amendment, the refusal to provide funds for various overseas initiatives, myriad restrictions on defense expenditures that direct the president's position in arms control talks, and the Boland Amendment in its various forms, have all been intended to restrict the ability of the executive branch to conduct the foreign affairs of this country.

The Iran/Contra committees and their joint hearings represented the pinnacle of that effort. The hearings were clearly calculated to criminalize executive foreign policies carried out without the support or knowledge of Congress. If the committees succeed in their ultimate objective, the revolution in the relations between Congress and the presidency in foreign policy will be legitimized, with profound implications for the future of our national security.

When the Iran arms sale and Contra diversion stories first broke in November 1986, there was little doubt in Washington that another impeachment-style scandal was in the making. Both houses of Congress launched investigations and created separate committees.

The Senate committee's staff was officially nonpartisan. Chief Counsel Arthur Liman had a reputation as an effective defense lawyer whose high-powered clients included Robert Vesco, John Zaccaro, and Carl Icahn. Assistant Counsel Paul Barbadoro had worked on Warren Rudman's legal staff when the senator was New Hampshire's attorney general. The House staff, though, was separated along partisan lines; the chief counsel was John Nields, whose reputation was earned on the Ethics Committee's Koreagate investigation. The ranking Republican, Congressman Dick Cheney, chose a member of his subcommittee's legal staff, George Van Cleve, as chief minority counsel.

Inevitably Conflicts Arose

Eventually the two committees agreed to conduct their hearings jointly, but the differences in staff organization meant that they could not be completely merged. It is remarkable that the staffs worked together as well as they did, conducting joint interviews and depositions and sharing the fruits of their investigatory work.

The parallel investigation by the independent counsel, Lawrence Walsh, did create problems, though. Walsh's purpose was to determine whether criminal prosecutions should be pursued. The committees' purpose, in response to a political crisis, was to examine the "process" of foreign policy formulation and to publicize the facts. This created conflicts between the committees' need for expedition and the special prosecutor's need for secrecy and time-consuming thoroughness.

Inevitably the conflicts arose. The independent counsel blocked the committees' access to certain

Dennis Teti, "The Coup That Failed," *Policy Review*, Fall 1987. Reprinted with permission.

Department of Justice documents. He claimed the privilege of reviewing the committees' materials but would not, or legally could not, reciprocate. Moreover, Walsh pressured the committees to delay granting "use immunity" to Oliver North, John Poindexter, and others. His confidence in the case against North could not have been high when he asked the committees in June—six months into his investigation—not to grant immunity to North at all. But to close the hearings without the key figure's testimony would have discredited the congressional examination, and Walsh was turned down.

The combined staffs, numbering over 100, were the engine of the investigation. They reviewed some 250,000 documents and selected those needed for further examination. The counsels and staffs privately interviewed and took depositions from approximately 500 witnesses, far more than appeared on camera, and they also prepared most of the questions the members asked during the hearings. Some members seemed hardly more than mouthpieces for young, committed staffers.

The direction of the investigation was largely the responsibility of the Senate's chief counsel, assisted by the House counsel and the chairmen. A few days past the 30th anniversary of Senator Joseph McCarthy's death, his spirit seemed alive and well in the Senate's Russell caucus room. As a Harvard student in 1954, Arthur Liman had written that ". . . congressional investigating committees pose not just a challenge to the relatively few individuals who appear before them but to the whole concept of limited government." But in the Iran/Contra hearings, Counsel Liman began his cross-examination with a scathing attack on the first witness, General Richard Secord. The inquisitional tone of the hearings was established from the very beginning.

Questionable Tactics

General Secord, appearing voluntarily, had infuriated some senators by successfully challenging in federal court a Senate subpoena of his financial records. Senator David Boren, a frequent defender of the "rule of law," launched into a harsh interrogation designed to punish Secord, notwithstanding the Senate's loss at the bar. Boren grilled Secord about his financial interests with certain dubious individuals, and concluded by trying to embarrass Secord into signing away his rights to remaining funds in Albert Hakim's Swiss bank accounts that had been set aside for the Contra resupply operation. Secord's stout resistance to this bullying generated early public displeasure with the committees' tactics. Any pretense that the hearings were examining "process" rather than policy, airing "facts" and not criminal charges, disappeared that first day.

The committees' counsels were not above using misleading and questionable tactics against witnesses. A well-known example occurred when Senate counsel, knowing Oliver North's family has been threatened by terrorists, placed a large exhibit of a North letter before the cameras, prominently featuring his home address. A second example was Chief Counsel Liman's one-page exhibit of the Boland Amendment, which was cropped to look as if it had been signed by Ronald Reagan as a separate law. The exhibit, reminiscent of the famed "cropped photograph" of the McCarthy hearings, was reconstructed from a nearly 2,000-page appropriations bill, and Liman had to suffer the indignity of being reproved by several committee members.

> "The committees' counsels were not above using misleading and questionable tactics against witnesses."

Counsels' chief instrument for pinning down witnesses was the private sworn deposition. Often requiring many hours of testimony and hundreds of pages, the depositions allowed counsel to explore leads and drop them, and they were often classified. Consequently, counsels and members who reviewed them knew exactly what answers would be given in public to leading questions, while witnesses could not change their story without risking perjury charges. Nor could witnesses always return to the depositions of themselves or others since that testimony was sometimes classified.

Oliver North's attorney, Brendan Sullivan, brilliantly exploited the committees' manipulations by challenging their right to take North's testimony privately and then again publicly. North obtained an agreement disguised as a "letter of intention" under which the committee took a deposition from him privately on only one subject. One major reason North's public appearance was so successful was that the committees had signed away their favorite instrument and counsels did not have sufficient time to make their best case against him.

In a February 1987 strategy memo, Liman had proposed that, except for the policymakers, North testify last. By then the committees would have explored the Iran/Contra story's details. Of the central witness Liman wrote: "If called, Colonel North would be immunized—but not against the rigorous cross-examination he would have to undergo by the senators in full view of the American people." It is hard to resist the conclusion that North's public indictment and punishment were among the committees' aims. If so, they were usurping both executive and judicial functions and transgressed the only legitimate reason for congressional investigations—fact-finding for legislative purposes.

The clearly adversarial nature of these proceedings reflected political divisions on four different levels: a partisan division between Democrats and Republicans; the split between the Senate and the House of Representatives; the deep dispute over U.S. policy in Central America and, implicitly, around the world; and most important, the profound constitutional struggle between the legislature and the executive to dominate foreign policy.

Party Shots

The partisan division over the Iran/Contra issues was the most obvious, but also the most superficial, of the differences within the committees. Democrats wasted little time trying to exploit the Reagan administration's embarrassment over the tangled Iran/Contra initiative. The Democratic leaders—visions of Watergate dancing in their heads—insisted on the congressional investigations, believing they could once again parade a cast of Haldemans, Deans, and Liddys before the disgusted eyes of the American electorate.

While it was apparent that partisan interests underlay the demand for the investigations, the party split was at first submerged. Committee votes on substantive and procedural matters in open and closed sessions reflected no partisan division; many were unanimous. The chairman and vice-chairman, in each case a Democrat and a Republican respectively, cooperated and coordinated their procedures and rules without any strong disagreements.

House Committee Chairman Lee Hamilton, despite strongly held neo-isolationist views, earned unanimous respect for his fair conduct of the hearings. Hamilton worked the compromise that averted a divisive committee vote and allowed Oliver North to give the spoken part of his Contra briefing on television.

"It became evident that Americans sympathized with the witnesses."

When partisan differences finally came to the fore, much of the controversy centered around Senate Chairman Daniel Inouye, a Democrat from Hawaii. Inouye's reputation from Watergate days for balance and nonpartisanship was tarnished by his personal attacks on witnesses implying that Oliver North resembled a Nazi war criminal and that he was trying to override the Constitution by requesting dispensation from a *pro forma* 48-hour committee rule on opening statements.

One example of Inouye's egregious partisanship came on a television talk program where he

announced that his committee acquired a Poindexter memorandum that suggested that President Reagan might have been briefed on plans for a diversion of Iranian arms sales profits. There were two problems with Inouye's statement. First, the memo he referred to said nothing about a diversion. Second, Inouye knew at the time of his appearance that Poindexter, in his private deposition, had absolved President Reagan of such knowledge, yet Inouye misled the audience into believing the question remained in doubt.

The partisan differences crystallized when it became evident that Americans sympathized with the witnesses and began criticizing the committees for unfair treatment. The Republicans, especially from the House, became more aggressive and confrontational as public support for the cause of the Contras increased, a development that shocked the Democrats.

Hyperbolic Senate, Crisp House

Lines of division at the hearings were also clearly drawn between House and Senate. The Senate committee frequently appeared to be nonpartisan to a degree the House panel never tried to be. This was reflected in the ways in which the two committees organized their staffs. Senator Rudman, the vice-chairman, and Senators Cohen and Trible adopted the Howard Baker model of independence and distanced themselves from the White House. In questioning witnesses they were often in greater sympathy with their Senate Democratic colleagues than with White House Republicans. Senator McClure charted a course allowing him to expose Israel's involvement, while Senator Hatch, the president's most consistent defender, was usually the only Republican senator willing to risk a partisan posture. The House Republicans, on the other hand, had been specially chosen by Minority Leader Bob Michel for their allegience to the president and the party's policies, and for their willingness to engage in principled combat. . . .

Congress' Contra Diction

The committees were . . . divided on the substantive issue of support for the Contras. The Iran initiative by itself would not have led to a congressional inquiry because until the so-called "diversion" of the Iranian arms profits became known, there were no "improprieties" (President Reagan's word) to be investigated. It was the diversion that revived hopes, or fears, that Americans faced another presidential scandal.

The Contra policy, centerpiece of the Reagan Doctrine of encouraging democratic liberation movements within countries under Soviet domination, has sharply divided Congress throughout Reagan's presidency. Funding for the Contras passed in some years, failed in others, was forbidden some times, and provided with strings attached at other times, depending on how firmly the president made his case to the people. The votes have usually been very close.

Senate Counsel Liman had written that congressional investigative committees are frequently created to force a policy change on the executive. The basic policy purpose behind the hearings undeniably was to weaken public support for the Reagan policy of Contra assistance by criminalizing those who supported it after Congress' rejection.

A majority of both committees, including all the Republicans and six Democrats, had voted for Contra funding in 1986. But Democrats who had voted for Contra funds did so against their party's official positions, compelled by their particular constituencies. Congressman Les Aspin's was the most interesting case. By trying to project himself as a moderate pro-defense Democrat, Aspin nearly lost the chair of the Armed Services Committee because of his 1986 vote. He barely retained it by promising liberal Democrats he would vote "no" the next time.

Democrats who support the Contras could be relieved of their colleagues' reproach if they could use the illegitimacy or criminality of Contra assistance as an excuse. The vehicle for that relief was the Boland Amendment, which, in its various versions, had the effect of prohibiting certain executive agencies from using government appropriations for Contra military assistance for two years.

Ambiguous Boland Amendment

But the issues involved in Boland and related legislation were highly technical and complex, and the committees never came close to agreeing on a single interpretation. One problem was that the language, deliberately or not, did not incorporate an across-the-board prohibition. As Congressman Jim Courter pointed out, the Arms Export Control Act, by contrast, says simply, "No U.S. funds shall be expended. . . ." Nor were criminal penalties attached to Boland.

Second, while the prohibition applied to "any agency or entity involved in intelligence activity," there was strong disagreement among committee members as to whether the National Security Council [NSC] was covered. It was learned that within the administration, too, there was considerable disagreement, even within the Council. Robert McFarlane, NSC advisor in 1985, testified that he believed Boland did not restrict the National Security Council, but that his belief was a matter of policy, not law. Admiral Poindexter, McFarlane's successor, believed the opposite. The only White House legal document to address the issue was a memo from the president's Intelligence Oversight Board, which took the position that "the NSC was not covered by the prohibition."

Third, if the National Security Council was included within the prohibition, its status as part of the president's personal staff would raise profound constitutional difficulties regarding Congress' powers to prevent the president from using his staff to carry out foreign policy operations.

Adding to the confusion, President Reagan protested that his administration always operated within the law—implying that Boland was the law—then later asserted that he was not covered by Boland. The administration never advanced a coherent position on the amendment.

"On the deepest level the Iran/Contra dispute is constitutional, part of a permanent contest between Congress and the president for control over foreign policy."

The committees claimed only to be examining the "process" of foreign policy formulation and operations within the executive branch; but committee Republicans never accepted that artificial limitation on the range of pertinent subjects. From the first witness, General Secord, to the last, the substance of the Contra support policy was kept in clear focus by the Republicans. Anti-Contra Democrats at first tried not to engage in policy debate, but the Republicans' determined pro-Contra speeches began to gain favorable public response even before Oliver North's impassioned testimony. When the House Chairman Hamilton quietly inserted polling data in the record purporting to support the opponents of Contra aid, the effort to suppress the policy debate ended.

Anti-Contra members faced a difficult problem: Although the witnesses had contradicted each other on many facts, they unanimously agreed that Congress should continue the assistance that had finally been voted [in 1986]. Many took Congress to task for the two-year hiatus.

It was in this context that Senate Counsel Liman made a serious tactical blunder. Questioning Lt. Colonel North about a slide briefing he often gave in which he graphically described Sandinista oppression and the Contras' determined struggle for democracy, Liman accused him of giving a pitch in order to solicit private contributions—arguably a violation of Boland. Congressmen Hyde, Courter, Cheney, and other Republicans seized on Liman's mistake and forced Chairman Inouye to allow North to present the entire briefing in the caucus room. Though unable to use his slides, North's 20-minute verbal description, according to polling data, substantially boosted popular support for the Contras. At the end of the hearings, only Chairman Inouye, in acerbic closing remarks to North, expressed opposition to the Contra aid program.

The increase in support for the Contras' cause following the testimony of North and others was one of the ironic but genuine benefits of the much-publicized hearings, which amounted to the most extensive debate most Americans have ever heard on the issue. Although Donald Regan testified to the president's determination to "drive [the Sandinista] government out of there," the administration has never expressed that view in public. It may yet turn out that North, his "courier" Robert Owen, and former superior Admiral Poindexter, by unapologetically taking their case to the people in a way that President Reagan never did, may have twice saved the Nicaraguan democratic resistance.

War Between the Branches

On the deepest level the Iran/Contra dispute is constitutional, part of a permanent contest between Congress and the president for control over foreign policy. Again and again, committee members appealed to the image of "co-equal partners" to legitimize congressional intervention in the foreign policy "process."

Congress has a genuine but subordinate role to play in the formulation of foreign policy. Neither the intentions of the Constitution's drafters, traditional theories of democratic government, nor common sense suggest that the executive branch should be given a completely free hand in this area. But as Congress increasingly insists on the *equality* of its powers, it is forgetting the Constitution's fairly clear differentiation of *function*. Among the slogans the committees appealed to, none were more favored than "checks and balances," and the talismanic claim of "equal partners." This sloganeering begs the question of what Congress' proper role in foreign policy should be.

"There are . . . obvious reasons why foreign policy should be lodged primarily within the executive."

A close look at the Constitution shows that, while the executive branch does not possess the entirety of foreign policy power, it has most of it. Under Article II, "executive power" is lodged in the president. By definition the executive power comprehends the conduct of foreign policy. The Framers found it unnecessary to define the term, but the inclusion of foreign policy under executive power is discussed at length in John Locke's *Two Treatises of Government*, a fundamental source for the Founders. The briefest review of legal and political documents from the late

18th century demonstrates that most political theorists of the era thought foreign policy to be executive in nature.

Where the Framers rejected absolute separation of powers, for example by giving the Senate the power of ratifying treaties and advising and consenting to executive branch appointments, and the power to declare war, they said precisely that these were *exceptions* to the general constitutional principle of separation. Where no exception is specified, the principle holds.

There are some obvious reasons why foreign policy should be lodged primarily within the executive, and they apply more forcefully in the latter 20th century than they did in the 18th. The conduct of foreign affairs often requires expeditious action around the globe. The processes of congressional deliberation, while providing useful input for the president in his formulation of long-range policy goals, are too slow and cumbersome to be of value for such decisions. Congress' inability to keep secrets was well-understood by the Founders, and the undeniable problem of congressional leaks was an important issue addressed by the hearings. Only a single executive can make foreign policy decisions swiftly and, when necessary, secretly, and he must do so within the framework of a coherent and principled foreign policy.

Almost invariably, the president will have submitted his foreign policy to the national electorate for ratification. As the architects of the Constitution expected, few congressmen run on such issues, and typically they are more sensitive in office to the local interests and needs of their constitutents than to the national interest as a whole.

In the past, these reasons were enough to prevent Congress from encroaching upon executive prerogatives. For a number of reasons the traditional arguments no longer appear sufficient, but the central difficulty is Congress' concern with bureaucracy.

Congress Evades Its Duty

Bureaucratic government became a major problem for American democracy with the New Deal. The founders of the science of administration such as Woodrow Wilson acknowledged that nonpolitical bureaucracies would threaten democracy unless democratic controls were placed on the administrative agencies. That task naturally fell to the Congress, and as a result the legislature now primarily occupies itself not with making law about domestic problems but with the unending task of administrative "oversight"—a function never mentioned in the Constitution.

Congress extended its oversight claim into the foreign policy domain of the executive as that area also became bureaucratized in the State Department, the Central Intelligence Agency, the National

Security Council, and other agencies. Congress' solution to foreign policy problems is typically more bureaucracy—more formal procedures, division of bureaucratic functions into separate entities, greater input and review from more agencies and divisions, and, above all, further participation in the decision-making process by Congress and the designated oversight committees.

The criminalization of foreign policy differences, which was the theme of the Iran/Contra hearings, is a further extension of Congress' longtime effort to suppress the political differences between itself and the president and to dominate another part of the federal bureaucracy.

The question is, how are the chief executive and his staff to be held accountable? How are we to control the Colonel Norths and Admiral Poindexters of the future unless Congress exercises an oversight function? The Constitution provides several methods that remain valid after 200 years.

The president of the United States is the responsible officer for the executive branch. As soon as North's and Poindexter's actions were brought to light—by the attorney general, not by Congress—they were dismissed. Service at the pleasure of the president is one effective control.

Second, presidents are held accountable for their foreign policy record as well as their administrative management every four years through the fundamental democratic check of periodic elections. In addition, members of Congress have sometimes litigated their differences with presidents in the U.S. Supreme Court. Recently 107 congressmen brought suit against President Reagan to force him to invoke the War Powers Resolution as respects naval operations in the Persian Gulf.

"The criminalization of foreign policy differences, which was the theme of the Iran/Contra hearings, is a further extension of Congress' longtime effort to . . . dominate another part of the federal bureaucracy."

Finally, presidents and other executive officials can be impeached by Congress for serious crimes. One of the most serious offenses against the United States is violation of the president's oath to "preserve, protect, and defend" the Constitution, one of the important sources of the executive power over foreign policy.

Congress shrinks from its obligation to impeach executive officers because the members want at all costs to avoid a divisive vote on a president's activities. Oversight hearings by standing or select committees such as the Iran/Contra panels enable Congress to evade the duty of impeachment by attacking instead administrative processes and "rogue bureaucrats" like North and Poindexter. The obvious political desirability of avoiding impeachment proceedings is one of several important reasons why members of Congress have little incentive to weaken bureaucratic government. But the political seriousness of impeachment shows how important the Framers thought it was for the chief executive to have great latitude in the operation of foreign policy.

Disregard for the constitutional division of powers that was designed by the Framers to prevent tyranny is a deeply troubling problem for the future of democratic freedom. Congressional oversight of executive agencies within a bureaucratized government cannot be avoided. But the unprecedented problems we confront around the world make it imperative for Americans to reconsider the value of an administrative state that saps our ability to rule ourselves democratically. The micro-management of areas in which Congress cannot play more than a minimal role is fast approaching the dimensions of a constitutional crisis. . . .

The Prosecution Folds

As soon as the members began to hear that their constituents were supporting Oliver North, the prosecutory phase of the hearings ended. Senate Counsel Liman's leonine roaring was reduced to feline purring—though no one was fooled, least of all the witness and his attorney. After North's impassioned defense of the Nicaraguan resistance, member after member protested support for Contra assistance. Only Congressman Jack Brooks (whose 35 years of seniority create an aura of political invulnerability) dared attack North openly; but I am certain that many, especially on the Senate side, boiled with indignation at North's bold defense of executive prerogative and legislative subordination in the foreign policy arena. Senator Rudman, for example, tried pathetically to praise Secretary of State George Shultz as "a *real* hero," implying that North's popularity was fraudulent.

The waning of the committees' hopes was symbolized when Liman, after a day's questioning of North, threw up his hands in despair and said he could not question a witness whose lawyer interrupted every question. Once Admiral Poindexter, following North, revealed publicly that he had concealed the diversion from President Reagan, the committees' long-range political intention seemed to collapse. Supported by millions of Americans, the witnesses had overwhelmed the committee.

Chairman Hamilton's concession came in his closing speech on August 3 when he said, "The solution to the problems of decision-making revealed in these hearings lies less in new structures or new laws than in proper attitudes." Had the hearings succeeded in their political and constitutional objectives, they would not have been satisfied with new "attitudes." They would have institutionalized Congress' demand to co-determine foreign policy.

At the end, the remaining witness list was drastically pared to a handful of policymakers, the questioning had attenuated, and the committees raced to complete their work and the final report. They decided to ask a number of foreign policy "wise men" to propose possible recommendations and remedies. Ultimately, then, apart from the committees' leaders, the members neither directed the investigation nor led the questioning nor controlled the evidence nor wished to create solutions to the problems the panels were established to recommend. They were intimidated by the popularity of a Marine Corps lieutenant colonel who had been fired from the NSC for possible "improprieties," and hardly ventured to challenge any witness after him.

Eight months before, these same members of Congress were demanding greater say in the conduct of foreign policy. How a Congress that could not muster the courage to challenge the political standing of an Ollie North could expect to stand up to the Gorbachevs, Castros, and Ortegas of our world, was a question for which the Iran/Contra hearings offered no answer.

Constitutional Turning Point?

I believe no committee investigation has had so little public sympathy since the McCarthy hearings over 30 years ago. The failure of the hearings to generate deep anti-Reagan sentiment and support for congressionally favored isolationism could mark the beginning of Congress' retreat from its 15-year effort to seize the initiative in foreign affairs. . . .

The Framers of our Constitution designed the Congress to be the seat of cool deliberation. The calm quality of prudence that is so necessary to the art of legislation has been replaced by its opposite, heated moral indignation.

"The failure of the hearings to generate deep anti-Reagan sentiment and support for congressionally favored isolationism could mark the beginning of Congress' retreat."

The replacement of deliberation with moral indignation is one consequence of the substitution of oversight for legislation, and it has made the consideration of rational policy alternatives difficult if not impossible. Anger is an essential support for the legal enforcement of justice in the community, but it is no substitute for clear thought in choosing the ends and means of public policy. This is not the least of reasons why, after months of televised hearings, the Iran/Contra committees failed to impress the public. The American people wait for more serious solutions to the threat posed by our implacable Communist adversaries who have never paused in their struggle to secure a beachhead on the American continent.

Dennis Teti was a member of the Iran-contra committees' staff.

Covert Operations Are Justifiable

George A. Carver Jr.

The Iran-Contra hearings, now mercifully ended, make one think of Shakespeare. To paraphrase Mark Anthony (in *Julius Caesar*), the evil men do lives after them, the good is oft interred with their reports. Even more pertinent, particularly in the aftermath of the hearings, is Lady Macduff's plaint (in *Macbeth*) at being:

> In this earthly world, where to do harm
> Is often laudable; to do good, sometime
> Accounted dangerous folly

These Shakespearean aphorisms apply with particular force to something much-debated in the hearings but little understood, inside or outside the hearing room—or even, alas, in the Reagan White House: covert action.

Successful foreign policy, as Alexis de Tocqueville observed, requires secrecy and patience. Washington abounds in neither, at either end of Pennsylvania Avenue, which is far from the least reason why many of our foreign policy ventures are notably unsuccessful.

Covert Action Necessary

Covert action is a special, often useful and sometimes essential form of secret diplomacy, practiced from time immemorial by all manner of tribes, kingdoms and nations to further their interests and those of their friends or allies, or thwart the designs of their adversaries, in situations where it is deemed desirable or necessary to mask the hand of the action in question's true instigator or sponsor.

Before we condemn this as invariably sinister, we should remember that we never would have won our war of independence and become a free nation without French and Spanish covert action support, initially handled with great secrecy to keep the donors themselves from becoming openly embroiled in a direct conflict with George III's Britain.

We also should remember that, for similar reasons, private individuals often act in a similar fashion. A benign mother or aunt who tries "to bring two young people together" without being an obvious matchmaker is engaging in covert action, as is anyone who tries to break up an alliance that person considers ill-advised, without getting counterproductively caught in the process.

There are many similarities between covert action and a scalpel. Neither can be wielded successfully by a committee.

Like covert action, a scalpel is useful, even essential in certain situations, though disaster can result quickly if it is not skillfully employed, with a deft and sure hand, by someone who knows what he is doing. Surgeons do not forgo scalpels because if inappropriately or clumsily used they can inflict great injury, even cause death.

Similarly, covert action—despite the risks its employment engenders—is a tool of statecraft no nation should forgo, and very few do.

In dealing with the United States, for example, virtually every nation in the world supplements its open diplomacy with various forms of covert action—or unadvertised, unacknowledged lobbying—attempting, with varying degrees of success, to influence our opinions and actions in ways congenial to the nation in question's perception of its interests. Our adversaries are by no means the only ones to essay this game; indeed, no one plays it more indefatigably, or successfully, than one of our closest allies—Israel.

Rules for Covert Actions

To stand any reasonable chance of being successful, a proposed or contemplated covert action must meet several tests.

Conceptually, it should reflect a sense of

George A. Carver Jr., "Covert Action an Essential Form of Diplomacy," *Human Events*, December 12, 1987. Reprinted with permission.

proportion and perspective. Immediate desires and objectives—such as freeing hostages—never should be allowed to obscure or put at risk larger, long-term national interests, such as punishing and curbing terrorism. It also should be sensible, running with—never against—the grain of local reality in the area in which the operation in question is to be attempted.

Like surgery, covert action should be conducted by trained, experienced professionals, not entrusted to zealous, well-meaning amateurs with more energy than judgment, whose warheads are better than their guidance systems.

By definition, no covert action should be undertaken unless there is a reasonable chance of keeping it secret, and no such action should be conducted in a way that increases its risk of exposure. Secrecy being hard to maintain under the best of circumstances, however, the political and other costs of exposure should be assessed carefully before a final decision is made to launch any given covert action operation.

Though covert action operations—again, by definition—inevitably involve at least some dissimulation and deception, no such operation should be basically inconsistent or incompatible with any important, publicly proclaimed government policy.

Covert action functions at the margins of policy—ideally, in a quietly supportive way. It can contribute, sometimes significantly, to a policy's success, but it can never be an effective substitute for policy—or for thought. Furthermore, the most brilliantly conceived and skillfully executed covert action operation cannot salvage or redeem a policy that is fundamentally unsound or flawed.

Spoiling a Good Policy

Providing U.S. arms to Iran, by the planeload, in a feckless effort to negotiate the release of American hostages for these already provided arms, failed every test and violated every precept just outlined.

From an American perspective (though not necessarily from an Israeli one), the Iranian exercise was a disastrous fiasco—particularly as a covert action operation.

At its end, Iran's stock of weapons and resultant military capabilities were increased markedly (which may well have been Israel's primary objective), the Reagan Administration and the United States were gravely embarrassed, the sound American policy of not negotiating with terrorists was undercut badly, and the number of American hostages held in or near Lebanon by Shiite militant factions presumably responsive to Iranian influence, such as Hezbollah, had not diminished, but, instead, had increased by half (from six in the summer of 1985 to nine in the summer of 1987).

In the process, matters were worsened by grafting the Iran exercise onto the Contra support and resupply endeavor (another Israeli suggestion)—thus violating every professional canon of compartmentation and sound security in running covert action operations, with the inevitable result any professional could have predicted. This was doubly unfortunate, since the Contra endeavor was far more sensible and defensible, on its merits, than the Iran quadrille and never should have been tarred with the latter's brush.

As a candidate for election, then reelection, and as President, Ronald Reagan never has made any secret of the fact that he considers the establishment of a Cuban- and Soviet-supported Communist dictatorship in Central America, in Nicaragua, a potential threat to America's vital interests.

"Washington should focus on protecting our nation's . . . capabilities—including covert action capabilities."

Whatever its defects in detailed conception and in execution, the Contra-aid endeavor directly supported—and, unlike the Iran exercise, did not undercut or contravene—well-known, often-enunciated Reagan Administration policy.

In retrospect, it was, nonetheless, clearly not wise or politically astute to handle Contra aid as a covert action operation. Indeed, 20-20 hindsight strongly suggests that the country and Congress, as well as the Administration, would have been far better served if Lt. Col. Oliver North—in open session, with appropriate publicity—had given Congress his forceful presentation of the case for Contra aid in 1982, before the passage of the first of the five "Boland amendments," not at a post-Iran-Contra disaster hearing in 1987.

Interbranch Struggle

We cannot go back, however, only forward. We should do so, furthermore, in the realization that ample mistakes already have been made, at both ends of Pennsylvania Avenue.

Mining these errors for partisan political advantage should not be anyone's primary objective. Instead, the American people and their elected representatives in Washington should focus on protecting our nation's interests, the capabilities—including covert action capabilities—that any administration, of any party, will need to safeguard.

Unfortunately, no such focus is evident currently on Capitol Hill, or in the White House. Instead, there is only sharp skirmishing in the unending legislative-executive branch struggle for foreign policy primacy, a struggle as old as our republic and ingrained in our Constitution—which, by design, divides this power as well as others.

Perceiving presidential weakness, a partisan Congress is pressing to extend its prerogatives, while an embarrassed, beleaguered White House seems willing, even eager, to placate Congress by voluntarily accepting self-imposed restrictions that Ronald Reagan and his Oval Office successors one day may regret bitterly.

In this situation, both Congress and the White House—as well as America's media and public— would profit from recalling some pertinent history.

Covert Actions in History

With little congressional knowledge and even less congressional input, President Thomas Jefferson's representatives—Robert Livingston and James Monroe—negotiated the Louisiana Purchase from Napoleon, who shrewdly sold them land he could not defend. The treaty consummating this purchase was signed in Paris on April 30, 1803, and ratified by a somewhat surprised Senate the following November.

Thus, for an eventual total price of $27,267,622, Jefferson—without any explicit constitutional warrant to do so—acquired a block of territory five times the size of France in area, and extended America's frontier westward to the Rockies.

With equally minimal congressional knowledge or input, Jefferson's successor, James Madison, directed the covert action operations that brought "West Florida" into the Union—i.e., the land extending to the east bank of the Mississippi, encompassing what is now Alabama and Mississippi, plus part of Louisiana, as well as Florida proper.

If Jefferson, the drafter of our Declaration of Independence, or Madison, the principal architect of our Constitution, had shown as President the diffident deference to Congress it is now fashionable to claim that a President is constitutionally obligated to show in conducting foreign affairs, our republic would not now have its present territorial extent and probably would not have survived its perilous initial decades.

Precedents even older than our republic are germane to current concerns and debates about covert action and about secrecy.

Our first foreign intelligence and covert action directorate—the Committee of Secret Correspondence—was established by the Continental Congress in November 1775. That committee negotiated and handled the covert French support without which we never could have won our struggle for independence.

Speaking of that support, two of the committee's members—Benjamin Franklin and Robert Morris— commented: "We agree in opinion that it is our indispensable duty to keep it a secret, even from Congress. . . . We find, by fatal experience, the Congress consists of too many members to keep

secrets." In this regard, little has changed in more than two centuries.

During the past two decades, the endemic, perpetual legislative-executive branch struggle over foreign policy has sharpened perceptibly—especially as Democratic-controlled Congresses, partly out of pique and frustration, have tried to hobble Republican Presidents, elected by landslides, and curtail their discretionary latitude.

In the process, Congress has attempted to insert itself into the management, even micro-management, of foreign affairs, thus asserting authority without accepting responsibility and essaying a role for which Congress not only has little constitutional warrant but also is ill-suited—by organization and temperament—to perform.

One example of this phenomenon is the 1973 War Powers Resolution, which President Nixon should have challenged immediately, on constitutional grounds, and probably would have had he not been mired in Watergate. It still needs to be challenged and, if possible, rescinded or struck down before a situation arises in which this act's potential for damage-causing mischief is fully realized. . . .

Other obvious examples are the five "Boland amendments" (one each in 1982, 1983 and 1984, then two in 1985), each of which was attached to an omnibus, veto-proof "continuing resolution" or spending bill made necessary by Congress' inability to complete its work on time.

Not one of these five amendments is clearly or precisely drafted, no two are consistent with each other, and the Reagan Administration should have challenged every one forcefully—particularly the first, when it initially was proposed—not tried to finesse or evade it after it was passed.

The Boland amendments symptomize and highlight a decidedly disquieting turn that legislative-executive branch struggles over foreign policy recently have taken: The attempt by Democratic congressional leaders and their media supporters to criminalize foreign policy differences.

"Congress has attempted to insert itself into the management, even micro-management, of foreign affairs."

This effort set a tone that permeated the Iran-Contra hearings, as evidenced by the Washington *Post*'s headline over its wrap-up story: "Three Months of Hearings Fail to Crack the Case."

Nothing but bitter divisiveness, damaging to a whole range of national interests, it likely to result from any continued effort to make differences of opinion over foreign policy into criminal matters to be resolved by the courts, rather than the subject of political debates to be settled at the ballot box.

The phenomenon of congressional assertiveness, with an attendant penchant for detailed, legalistic documentation, has been particularly pronounced in the sphere of covert action.

In 1974, the Hughes-Ryan Amendment to the Foreign Assistance Act of 1961 stipulated that the CIA [Central Intelligence Agency] could spend no funds "for operations in foreign countries, other than activities intended solely for obtaining necessary intelligence, unless and until the President finds that each such operation is important to the national security of the United States."

This requirement for reporting to the Congressional Intelligence Oversight Committees was broadened and tightened in the Intelligence Authorization Act for Fiscal Year 1981, though that act did leave the President the discretionary option of reporting sensitive covert action activities "in a timely fashion." The Reagan Administration clearly abused this option in its handling of the Iran-Contra matter, quite understandably irritating Congress in the process.

"There is a great danger that the covert action capabilities our nation urgently needs—for its security and perhaps even its survival—will be crimped, emasculated or erased."

Not surprisingly, given Congress' current mood and temper, several bills to tighten these restrictions even further already are in the hopper, including HR 1013—sponsored by House Intelligence Committee Chairman Louis Stokes and former Chairman Edward P. Boland, among others—that would require the circulation of additional copies of written presidential findings, eliminate the "in a timely fashion" provision, and require advance notice to Congress of all contemplated covert action operations, with but one, 48-hour exception to be used "only in extraordinary circumstances affecting the vital interests of the United States, and only where time is of the essence."

Similar ideas were reflected in "suggestions" given to the White House by the Senate's oversight committee, to which President Reagan responded in a disquieting August [1987] letter that the White House took pains to publicize. In the present situation, the White House's timorous defensiveness may be as understandable as congressional assertiveness, but both need to be curbed if the national interest is not to suffer.

What is also perhaps not surprising, but certainly regrettable, is that a similar mood seems to have afflicted the White House, where executive orders apparently are being written or revised to impose limitations on covert action that Congress has not yet formally requested or, even less, mandated.

Those who wrote, passed or issued the restrictions on covert action now in force forgot or ignored a unique, very important feature of our Constitution, which all those considering new restrictions should remember.

The Chief of State

Our Constitution combines in one individual, our President, two distinct offices and functions that virtually all other nations divide: the government's chief executive and administrative officer—a partisan political figure chosen (in America) by election—and the nation's chief of state—a symbolic focus of national unity, supposedly, in that capacity, above the fray of political partisanship.

As chief executive officer, a President certainly should be accountable for his and his administration's actions. Nonetheless, it is by no means necessarily in our national interest for our chief of state to sign "findings" or any other documents directing agencies or officers of the U.S. government to infringe upon or violate the laws of other nations with which we are not in a state of declared war.

National Security Council staff members, national security advisers, Cabinet officers and directors of Central Intelligence are all expendable, but in our government, Presidents are not.

As chief of state, an American President should be able to distance himself or herself from, even disavow, a covert action that he or she approved, even ordered, as chief executive. This may sound complicated, but so is the real world and, hence, effective diplomacy that runs with the grain of its complex reality.

With the White House taking the lead, the Administration obviously needs to reform and improve its relevant structures and mechanisms, and then use them—not ignore them or supplant them with hip pocket, *ad hoc* arrangements.

The Administration's relations and manner of dealing with Congress manifestly need to be improved; for no matter who may or may not like this arrangement, our Constitution yokes the legislative and executive branches in a single harness, and unless they can pull together, in tandem, the nation suffers.

To be effective, however, this kind of tandem-harness partnership requires reciprocal confidence and trust, which *both* partners must work to build and maintain—even when the White House is controlled by one party and Congress by another.

Additionally, there is much that Congress needs to do in the field of secrecy protection.

The current Senate and House Intelligence

Oversight committees, to cite another example, have a total of 32 members, plus four honorary members (the majority and minority leaders in each house), plus about 60 more people on the two committee staffs (combined). That makes a total of around a hundred people on Capitol Hill who, under existing arrangements, are formally, officially apprised of covert operations.

No matter how these committees' majorities may rule, any of these 100-odd people, members or staffers, can kill by a pre-emptive leak any covert action of which he or she personally disapproves. That is not a workable situation if a true covert action capability is to be preserved.

At a minimum, Congress should give serious consideration to combining these two separate oversight committees into one joint committee with an appreciably smaller membership and a much smaller combined staff.

Endangering a Tool of Statecraft

In the wake of the Iran-Contra hearings, the concerns and emotions that promoted them, and the additional emotions they engendered, there is a great danger that the covert action capabilities our nation urgently needs—for its security and perhaps even its survival—will be crimped, emasculated or erased by a new spate of restrictive laws and regulations hastily written in a fit of moralistic pique.

This might suffuse the drafters and enactors of such laws and regulations with a transient glow of self-righteous virtue, but for the country it would be disastrous. If this were to happen, harking back to Mark Anthony, the Iran-Contra committee—whatever its intent may have been—would have done evil that would live longer after that committee was disbanded and its various reports interred in files.

George A. Carver Jr. is a senior fellow at the Center for Strategic and International Studies in Washington, DC, and a former Central Intelligence Agency officer.

"Without noteworthy exception, the use of covert military action in support of American foreign policy has ended in failure or catastrophe."

Covert Operations Are Unjustifiable

Lewis H. Lapham

Incompetent armies deify the commander.
—Prussian maxim

While watching hearings before the Iran-*contra* committees, and again while reading the text of the congressional report, I kept expecting to hear somebody say something—not loudly, of course, and maybe only through a handkerchief, but at least something—about our slave's faith in secret wars. Surely, I thought, here was a chance to renounce both the theory and practice to covert action. About the practice, the politicians were often critical, a few of them permitting themselves an occasionally acerbic remark about the blundering dishonesty of Attorney General Edwin Meese and Vice Adm. John Poindexter. But on the point of doctrine the committees remained as silent as a colony of Christmas mice. Not once during the entire three months of testimony, or throughout the whole 690 pages of the published narrative, did anybody—not a single congressman, lawyer, or witness—utter so much as a single word against the fatuous and cynical belief that the cause of liberty can be made to stand on the pedestal of criminal violence.

A few members of the committees worried about what they called "the paradox" or "the contradictions" implicit in the waging of clandestine warfare under the jurisdiction of "a free, open, and democratic society." A few other members expressed the forlorn hope that covert actions might be limited in size and cost, or undertaken only with the written permission of the Congress. But in answer to any and all direct questions about the need to deal manfully with events not always to one's liking, all present bowed their heads and murmured in solemn unison, saying, in effect: "Yes, it is a very, very dangerous world, heavily populated with all sorts of

dangerous enemies armed with all sorts of dangerous weapons, and in order to defend ourselves against threats of infinite number we have no choice but to resort—reluctantly, of course, and ever mindful of the temporary damage to our constitutional principles—to murder."

Nobody ever failed to reaffirm his faith in this doctrine despite its proven stupidity. Asked to swear fealty to what amounted to Clint Eastwood's theory of diplomacy, the committees knelt and prayed.

So did the chorus of attending journalists and the choir of once and future statesmen. The editorials in the larger papers regretted the loss of the nation's innocence, but they reminded their readers that it was no good pretending that the world is a big, blue sandbox. Two former secretaries of state—Henry Kissinger and Gen. Alexander Haig—appeared on all three television networks to assure their audiences that secret operations were not only wonderfully effective but also, if properly conducted (i.e., by gentlemen as accomplished as themselves), entirely in keeping with the principles of Thomas Jefferson.

Covert Action a Failure

And yet, if somebody were to draw up a balance sheet reflecting the consequences of the covert actions we have let loose in the world over the last forty years, I expect that even a Pentagon accountant might concede the bankruptcy of the enterprise. Consistently and without noteworthy exception, the use of covert military action in support of American foreign policy has ended in failure or catastrophe. Whenever the United States embarks on one of those splendid little adventures so dear to the hearts of the would-be Machiavel[li]s in the White House or on the National Security Council, the patrol boats sink and the wrong tyrant seizes the palace and the radio station.

Unless the country stands willing to transform itself into a totalitarian state, even the theory of secret war is absurd. When mounted on any sort of large scale or extended over a period of more than two weeks, covert actions hide nothing from anybody except the people paying the bills. The Iran-*contra* hearings made it plain enough that the arms-for-hostages deals were known to several foreign governments (Israel, Iran, Saudi Arabia, Brunei, and Countries 8-16) as well as to an impressive crowd of Swiss bankers, Washington clerks, and Lebanese arms merchants.

Nor do the American operatives have much talent for covert action. The historical record is embarrassingly clear on the point. In the immediate aftermath of the Second World War, the earliest prototype of the CIA [Central Intelligence Agency], under the direction of Allen Dulles (a.k.a. "The Great White Case Officer"), enjoyed a brief moment of triumph in a world still largely in ruins, at a time when the military and economic supremacy of the United States went unquestioned by German waiters, and when it was possible to hire native gun-bearers for the price of a bar of chocolate and a pair of nylon stockings. The American intelligence services placed a number of agents behind Communist lines in Europe; recruited émigré armies to recapture the lost kingdoms of Poland, Bulgaria, and the Ukraine; and assisted with the removal of governments thought to be subversive in Iran (1953), Guatemala (1954), and the Philippines (1953).

Illusory Victories

Within a very few years the victories proved to be illusory or, at best, ambiguous. Advance scouts for the émigré armies parachuted into the Slavic darkness and were never seen or heard from again. By overthrowing a popular but socialist regime in Iran (at the behest of the Anglo-Iranian Oil Company), the United States opened the way to the vanity and ignorance of the Shah of Shahs (who had trouble speaking Farsi), to the quadrupling of the Arab oil price, the revolutionary zeal of the Ayatollah Khomeini, and the current impasse in the Persian Gulf.

The forced departure of Jacobo Arbenz from Guatemala (because his form of democratic socialism offended the United Fruit Company) allowed for the arrival of a notably vicious military junta, and in the Philippines the outfitting of Ramón Magsaysay with anti-Communist propaganda served as prelude to the corrupt regime of Ferdinand Marcos.

By the end of the decade, the American variations on themes of subversion had acquired the character of grotesque farce. With the hope of eliminating Achmed Sukarno as the president of Indonesia (because he permitted Communists to take their elected posts in his government), the CIA in 1957 armed a cadre of restless Sumatran colonels and engaged a Hollywood film crew to produce a pornographic film. Entitled *Happy Days*, the film

purportedly showed Sukarno (played by a Mexican actor wearing a mask) in bed with a Soviet agent (played by a California waitress wearing a wig). The coup d'état failed, and the film was understood as a joke.

In 1961 the bungled invasion at the Bay of Pigs (a.k.a. "the glorious march through Havana") ensured Fidel Castro's communist authority throughout Latin America. The subsequent attempts to assassinate him (at least five by the CIA's hired agents) quite possibly resulted in the assassination of John F. Kennedy.

Oriental Despotism

By encouraging the assassination of Ngo Dinh Diem in Saigon in 1963, the United States allied itself with a policy of realpolitik no less cynical than the one against which it was supposedly defending the principles of justice. Four American presidents defined the expedition in Vietnam as a prolonged covert action and systematically lied to the American people as to the reason for our presence in a country with which we never declared ourselves at war. As a result of our effort to rid Indochina of Communism, Vietnam became a unified Communist state. As a result of our effort to teach the world the lessons of democracy, we taught a generation of American citizens to think of their own government as an oriental despotism.

The discovery of the CIA's mining of the Nicaraguan harbors in 1983 obliterated the precarious advantage that the *contras* (on whose behalf the mines were placed) so desperately needed in the American Congress. Similarly discordant effects have followed our interventions in Cambodia, Angola, and Laos.

"So unequivocal a record of stupidity and failure begs the question as to why American officialdom persists in its idiot dream of invisible war."

So unequivocal a record of stupidity and failure begs the question as to why American officialdom persists in its idiot dream of invisible war. It isn't for lack of sound advice. The late Chip Bohlen, one of the wisest of American diplomats and once ambassador to Moscow, understood in the early 1950s that covert actions always take place at the not-very-important margins of not-very-important events. In 1961 President Dwight Eisenhower's Board of Consultants on Foreign Intelligence Activities reviewed the CIA's reputedly glorious record and was unable to conclude that "on balance, all of the covert action programs undertaken by the CIA up to this time have been worth the risk or the great expenditure of manpower, money, and other resources involved."

In the early years of the nineteenth century, John Quincy Adams took up the question of covert action and thought that America should send "her benedictions, and her prayers . . . wherever the standard of freedom and independence has been or shall be unfurled." But America doesn't send arms and munitions because "she goes not abroad in search of monsters to destroy."

Were America to embark on such a foolish adventure, Adams said, she would become entangled "beyond the power of extrication, in all the wars of interest and intrigue, of individual avarice, envy, and ambition, which assume the colors and usurp the standard of freedom. The fundamental maxim of [America's] policy would insensibly change from *liberty* to *force.* . . . She might become the dictatress of the world. She would no longer be the ruler of her own spirit."

"The theory and practice of covert military action inevitably subverts our own people as well as our institutions of government."

Arthur Schlesinger Jr. quotes Adams in the winter [1987/88] issue of *Foreign Affairs* and then goes on to quote John le Carré to the effect that covert actions recommend themselves to "declining powers," to men and institutions feeling the loss of their strength and becoming fearful of shadows. In le Carré's observation it is the timid and servile mind that places "ever greater trust in the magic formulae and hocus-pocus of the spy world. When the king is dying, the charlatans rush in."

Enter, to music for military band, Henry Kissinger, General Haig, Admiral Poindexter, Colonel [Oliver] North, and the braided company of Washington mountebanks, sophists, and leaping acrobats that drags behind it the wagons of the national security state. In the American context, the king is the spirit of liberty, which frightened and cynical people no longer know how to rule, and which, gratefully, they exchange for what they imagine to be the shields of their enemies.

Subverting the Nation

The theory and practice of covert military action inevitably subverts our own people as well as our institutions of government. The operatives in the employ of the White House or the intelligence agencies come to believe themselves surrounded by a host of evil spirits shrieking in a foreign wind. Paranoid and easily convinced of their virtue, they get in the habit of telling so many lies that they no longer know their friends from their enemies.

Hindsight, of course, is easier than foresight, but I wish that at least one member of the joint committees had taken the trouble to study the historical record and to raise his voice against the presiding superstition. I wish I wasn't so often reminded of a herd of docile cattle, lowing softly in a pasture, waiting for Clint Eastwood (or Admiral Poindexter or General [Richard] Secord or Colonel North) to lead them safely to slaughter.

Lewis H. Lapham is the editor of Harper's Magazine.

bibliography

The following bibliography of books, periodicals, and pamphlets is divided into chapter topics for the reader's convenience.

The US and Asia, Case Study: The Philippines

Robin Broad and John Cavanagh — "Our Wrong-Way Foreign Aid," *Los Angeles Times*, January 6, 1988.

William Chapman — *Inside the Philippine Revolution*. New York: W.W. Norton & Company, 1987.

Alexander Cockburn — "The Cory Myth," *The Nation*, September 19, 1987.

Solita Collas-Monsad — "Debt to Democracy," *The New Republic*, December 7, 1987.

Joseph Collins — "Cory's Broken Promise," *The Nation*, November 14, 1987.

Alan Cranston — "Let's Have a Marshall Plan for Philippines," *Los Angeles Times*, September 13, 1987.

Jason DeParle — "The Slum Behind the Sheraton," *The Washington Monthly*, December 1987.

James Fallows — "A Damaged Culture," *The Atlantic Monthly*, November 1987.

Richard J. Kessler — "Aquino Doesn't Have Much Time," *The New York Times*, November 6, 1987.

Louis Kraar — "Aquino Needs a New Miracle," *Fortune*, September 14, 1987.

Jim Mann — "Strength of Rebels Grows in Philippines," *Los Angeles Times*, February 29, 1988.

Anne Nelson — "In the Grotto of the Pink Sisters," *Mother Jones*, January 1988.

The New Republic — "Save Cory," November 2, 1987.

Stephen J. Solarz — "One Way To Shore Up Filipino Democracy," *The New York Times*, February 22, 1988.

Richard G. Stilwell — "Averting Disaster in the Philippines," *Policy Review*, Winter 1988.

Russell Watson — "The Military Choices Will Not Be Easy," *Newsweek*, February 22, 1988.

Simon Winchester — "Why Big Arrests Give Aquino Small Comfort," *U.S. News & World Report*, April 11, 1988.

The US and Central America, Case Study: Nicaragua

Harry Anderson — "Fallout from a Defector," *Newsweek*, December 28, 1987.

David Brock — "Sandinista Sweet Talk, Bitter Truth," *Insight*, November 30, 1987.

William F. Buckley Jr. — "Mrs. Kirkpatrick Visits Managua," *National Review*, November 20, 1987.

Commonweal — "A Never-Ending Process," February 26, 1988.

Congressional Digest — "Contra Aid: Pro and Con," March 1988.

Christopher J. Dodd — "Give the Arias Peace Plan a Chance," *The New York Times*, October 19, 1987.

David H. Gill — "Nicaragua: Some Necessary Distinctions," *America*, April 16, 1988.

Charles Krauthammer — "Whose Foreign Policy Is It, Anyway?" *Time*, February 8, 1988.

Robert Leiken — "Nicaragua Cliffhanger," *The New Republic*, December 14, 1987.

James LeMoyne — "Arias: Whom Can He Trust?" *The New York Times Magazine*, January 10, 1988.

T. Patrick Lynch — "Nicaraguan Perspectives," *America*, February 27, 1988.

Juan E. Mendez — "Should the Contras Be Newly Funded?: No, Because Human Rights Won't Benefit," *The New York Times*, February 1, 1988.

David Munro — *The Four Horsemen: The Flames of War in the Third World*. Secaucus, NJ: Lyle Stewart, 1987.

The Nation — "Ortega's Dilemma," November 21, 1987.

The New Republic — "Save the Contras," February 15, 1988.

Daniel Ortega Saavedra — "More Contra Aid, More Suffering," *The New York Times*, January 14, 1988.

Ernesto Palazio — "Should the Contras Be Newly Funded?: Yes, Because Democracy Would Gain," *The New York Times*, February 1, 1988.

The Progressive — "The Battle of the Isthmus," October 1987.

The Progressive — "The Nicaraguan Obsession," March 1988.

Ronald Radosh — "Nicaragua Revisited," *The New Republic*, August 3, 1987.

Ronald Reagan	"Central American Peace Plan," *Department of State Bulletin*, November 1987.
George Shultz	"Power in the Service of Peace in Central America," *Department of State Bulletin*, December 1987.
Jill Smolowe	"Tales of a Sandinista Defector," *Time*, December 21, 1987.
R. Emmett Tyrell, Jr.	"A Message from Miranda," *The American Spectator*, February 1988.
Lawrence Weschler	"The De-Meaning of Humanitarian Aid," *The Nation*, February 27, 1988.
Margaret D. Wilde	"Fighting the Sandinistas with Dollars," *The Christian Century*, November 4, 1987.

The US and the Middle East

Dale L. Bishop	"Two 'Nations of Hostages,'" *Christianity and Crisis*, March 16, 1987.
Hyman Bookbinder and James G. Abourezk	*Through Different Eyes: Two Leading Americans, a Jew and an Arab, Debate U.S. Policy in the Middle East*. Bethesda, MD: Adler and Adler, 1987.
Commentary	"American Jews and Israel—A Symposium," February 1988.
Amos Elon	"From the Uprising," *The New York Review of Books*, April 14, 1988.
Yaron Ezrahi	"Breaking the Deadlock: An Israeli View," *The New York Times Magazine*, February 21, 1988.
Hirsh Goodman	"Talk About Talks About Peace Plans," *U.S. News & World Report*, February 22, 1988.
John Greenwald	"Here a Mine, There a Mine," *Time*, August 24, 1987.
Tony Horwitz	"The Strait of Hommus," *The Washington Monthly*, March 1988.
Rich Jefferson	"Fighting to the Death for Mohammed's Faith," *Eternity*, June 1987.
Elie Kedourie	"Cruising for a Bruising: The U.S. in the Gulf," *The American Spectator*, October 1987.
Norman Kempster	"U.S. Gulf Policy Goals Met with No Calamities," *Los Angeles Times*, February 1, 1988.
Flora Lewis	"Stopping the Gulf War," *The New York Times*, March 23, 1988.
Scott MacLeod	"Search for Partners: Should the U.S. Deal with the Palestine Liberation Organization?" *Time*, April 11, 1988.
Richard W. Murphy	"The Persian Gulf: Stakes and Risks," *Department of State Bulletin*, July 1987.
The New Republic	"How To Defend the Gulf," June 22, 1987.
Amos Perlmutter	"Dissent on Iran," *The National Interest*, Winter 1987/1988.
Daniel Pipes and Laurie Mylroie	"Back Iraq," *The Nation*, April 27, 1987.
Nita M. Renfrew	"Who Started the War?" *Foreign Policy*, Spring 1987.
Mona Rishmawi	"Let Our People Go: What Palestinians Want," *The Nation*, March 19, 1988.
Micah L. Sifry	"After the 'Iron Fist'—What?" *The Nation*, February 13, 1988.
Michael Sterner	"Doing Something Right in the Gulf," *The New York Times*, January 27, 1988.

United States Department of State	"U.S. Policy in the Persian Gulf," July 1987. Special Report No. 166. Available from Bureau of Public Affairs, United States Department of State, Washington, DC, 20520.
Milton Viorst	"Letter from Jerusalem," *Mother Jones*, April 1988.
Caspar W. Weinberger	"The Military Underpinnings of Diplomacy: The Case of the Persian Gulf," *Vital Speeches of the Day*, November 1, 1987.
Tom Wicker	"Illusions Exploded in the Gulf," *The New York Times*, July 25, 1987.
Ronald J. Young	*Missed Opportunities for Peace: U.S. Middle East Policy, 1981-1986*. Philadelphia: American Friends Service Committee, 1987.

The US and the Middle East, Case Study: The Iran-Contra Affair

Dick Cheney	"What Needs Changing after Iran-Contra?" *The World & I*, February 1988.
Leslie Cockburn	*Out of Control*. New York: The Atlantic Monthly Press, 1988.
L. Gordon Crovitz	"Crime, the Constitution & the Iran-Contra Affair," *Commentary*, October 1987.
Theodore Draper	"An Autopsy," *The New York Review of Books*, December 17, 1987.
Theodore Draper	"The Rise of the American Junta," *The New York Review of Books*, October 8, 1987.
Henry Fairlie	"Curtain Call," *The New Republic*, September 7, 1987.
Harper's Magazine	"Hearing Nothing, Saying Nothing," February 1988.
William Hartung	"The Reagan Revival of Arms Deals," *Bulletin of the Atomic Scientists*, July/August 1987.
Henry J. Hyde	"Iran/Contra: Reality and Unreality," *National Review*, December 4, 1987.
Molly Ivins	"Profiteers and Loons," *The Progressive*, July 1987.
The Joint Congressional Committees	*The Iran-Contra Affair*. Washington, DC: Government Printing Office, 1987.
Jacob Lamar	"Conspiracy, Fraud, Theft and Cover-Up," *Time*, March 28, 1988.
Jonathan Marshall, Peter Dale Scott, Jane Hunter	*The Iran-Contra Connection*. Boston: South End Press, 1987.
The New Republic	"Saving Covert Action from Ollie North," August 3, 1987.
Gary North	"The Testimony of Lieutenant Colonel Oliver North," *Conservative Digest*, September 1987.
Warren Rudman	"Iran-Contra: What We Heard, What We Did," *Harper's Magazine*, April 1988.
I.F. Stone	"Covert Loophole," *The Nation*, September 5, 1987.
James Truab	"The Law and the Prophet," *Mother Jones*, February/March 1988.
Bob Woodward	*Veil: The Secret Wars of the CIA*. New York: Simon & Schuster, 1987.
World Press Review	"Cover Story: The Hearings," September 1987.

index